MEN'S MINISTRY
VOLUNTEER HANDBOOK

MEN'S
MINISTRY
VOLUNTEER HANDBOOK

Equipping You to Serve

First Edition: Year 2022
Men's Ministry Volunteer Handbook / Outreach, Inc.
Paperback ISBN: 978-1-951304-92-8
eBook ISBN: 978-1-951304-94-2

CHURCHLEADERS
PRESS

Colorado Springs

MEN'S
MINISTRY
VOLUNTEER HANDBOOK

Equipping You to Serve

Written by
Eric Jaqua

Content Editor
Mikal Keefer

Series Project Manager
Matt Lockhart

CHURCHLEADERS
PRESS

Colorado Springs

CONTENTS

INTRODUCTION

to the *Outreach Ministry Guides* Series

Each of you should use whatever gift you have received to serve others, as faithful stewards of God's grace in its various forms.
(1 Peter 4:10)

This handbook is part of a series designed to equip and empower church volunteers for effective ministry. If you're reading this, chances are you're a church volunteer. Thanks for your willingness to serve!

Several things make this handbook unique:
- The content is specific and practical for your given area of ministry.
- Experienced ministry practitioners—folks who've worked, served, and helped to train others in this particular area—compiled this information.
- It's written with you—a ministry volunteer—in mind.

Within these pages you'll find three sections. The first gives a brief overview of fundamental principles to provide you with a solid foundation for the ministry area in which you're serving.

Section 2 unpacks various skills related to the responsibilities involved. Understanding what is required and assessing if it's a good fit is helpful in creating a ministry team that is effective and serves together well.

Finally, Section 3 provides a multitude of practical ministry tools. These ideas and tips will help you demonstrate Jesus' love to the people you serve.

Whether you're a first-time volunteer or a seasoned veteran, my prayer is that the information and practical tools in this handbook will encourage and assist you. May God bless and guide you in your ministry!

—**Matt Lockhart,** Project Manager

to the Men's Ministry Volunteer Handbook

*S*o, you're serving in men's ministry....

First, thanks.

It's not a stretch to say that men's ministry may have saved my life. It's certainly true God used a men's ministry to pull me out of a dark, depressing hole I couldn't climb out of on my own.

When my then-wife filed for divorce, I needed an attorney. I asked around and within a few days was sitting in Mark's office, spilling out my story as he nodded and scratched a few notes on a yellow legal pad.

Mark finally raised a hand to stop my monologue.

"What are you doing tonight?" he asked.

I didn't know much about dealing with lawyers, but I knew a question like that wasn't usually part of the package. Was he thinking my case was so hopeless all he could do was take me out for a beer and call it good?

But it was a legitimate question. What *was* I doing that evening?

"I'm probably going back to my apartment to mope," I said, sounding pathetic even to myself.

Mark told me he met regularly with some Christian men who were getting together that evening. The group had just started reading and discussing *Wild at Heart*, a book by John Eldredge. He'd pick me up and I could come along.

I remember telling Mark I appreciated the offer but the last thing I wanted to do was sit in a room with men I didn't know discussing a book I hadn't read. Thanks, but no thanks.

If you've ever met someone whose enthusiasm can't be resisted, you've met Mark.

So that evening, after a 45-minute ride during which I half-wondered if I was being kidnapped, we walked into a kitchen where seven or eight guys were laughing and eating pizza.

I shook hands all around, grabbed a slice of pepperoni, and silently watched as these men—clearly all friends—checked in with one another. They knew what was happening in each other's lives and their concern for each other was genuine. They'd clearly given each other permission to ask hard questions and weren't afraid to be honest with each other.

What I saw—this friendship this fellowship—was different. Deep. And just what I needed. I decided on the spot I'd be coming back the next week.

I wasn't new to church or men's ministry. I'd gone to men's meetings and small groups in the past, but they always left me wanting more.

Conversations usually hovered around sports and current events. We seldom got beyond, "How you doing?" or "How's the family?" You could go to meetings for months and still not know more about the men than you'd known when they'd first introduced themselves.

That kind of shallow experience didn't satisfy me, so I didn't last in those groups. And usually the ministries themselves didn't last either.

But this kitchen group was something else. These men had gotten past the small talk and were connected, holding each other accountable and cheering one another on.

They were experiencing what you'll experience in your ministry as you apply the tips and ideas you'll find in this book. I've talked to some of the best men's ministry leaders I could find, and they've shared their wisdom. I've gathered stories that will show you how to miss ministry potholes and stay on solid ground.

As a men's ministry volunteer you impact not just the men you serve but their families as well. What happens in your meetings shifts how men approach marriage, raise their kids, and decide how to navigate balancing work and home lives.

It's no stretch to say what you do sends ripples through future generations.

I'm praying for you. Know that what you do matters and that God is using you in powerful ways.

—**Eric Jaqua**, Author

SECTION 1

MEN'S MINISTRY FOUNDATIONS

CHAPTER 1

WHY MEN'S MINISTRY

 $\mathcal{M}$ ost pastors will tell you one of their greatest challenges in working with a church body is ministering to the men.

Pastors would like to see a church full of godly men who know who they are in Christ, how they're wired for ministry, and why they need other men to encourage them and hold them accountable.

But most pastors quickly discover that they can't crack the code for how to reach and engage men. How to motivate men to grow. Or how to reach a place where that all-important accountability becomes the norm instead of the exception.

Reaching men is important because men are important—for more than one reason:

Because they influence their family's faith

If a child is the first person in a household to become a Christian, there's a 3.5 percent chance everyone else in the household will follow. If the mother is the first to follow Christ, there's a 17 percent chance the rest of the household will follow.

But if the *father* becomes a Christian first, there's a 93 percent chance everyone else in the household will follow Christ, too.[1]

A Swiss study revealed that if a father doesn't attend church, even if the mother is a faithful churchgoer, only one child in 50 will become a regular worshiper. But if a father attends church regularly,

---

1   *The Promise Keeper at Work*, Focus on the Family Publishing

regardless of the mother's attendance, between two-thirds and three-quarters of their children will attend church either regularly or occasionally.[2]

Even if you've never heard these statistics, the idea makes sense. As a volunteer in men's ministry you're aware that many more men—both within and beyond your church—could benefit from getting involved in your ministry.

And their families would benefit as well.

Because the church needs godly men

Yes, it's important to get men in the seats on Sunday mornings. But a healthy men's ministry does far more than assure that entire families attend services.

I watched how a healthy, growing men's ministry affected a local church. As our ministry grew from a small group, meeting in a home, into a few hundred men gathering in a church hall, I saw things change.

• **Men discovered their spiritual gifts** and looked to serve where they could serve best—and the church's ministries flourished.

• **Men stepped up in providing spiritual leadership in their homes**, prompting them to pay attention to and serve their spouses and children.

• **Men tamed the work beast**—making time to be with their families.

• **Men gladly discipled other men**, freeing up church staff to attend to other things.

At one meeting I was approached by a guy who admitted he'd planned to skip our weekly meeting. When he told his wife he intended to miss the meeting she told him—in no uncertain terms—

---

2   http://en.wikipedia.org/wiki/Church_attendance#Influence_of_
    parents

that he was *not* skipping the meeting, that he *would* be there, and he'd be there *on time*.

"Ever since you started hanging around with those wild men on Tuesday nights you've been a completely different man," she said. "I like what I see and love what's happening in you."

That's when we knew that what God was doing was way beyond anything we could see in our meetings. As men grow closer to God, that expresses itself at work, at home, everywhere.

That's also how our ministry got its name: *Wildmen*.

We could have done worse.

Because men need other godly men

Remember those National Geographic specials where you see a lion go after a herd of gazelles? The lion always targets a gazelle who's wandered away from the herd, who's isolated.

Ditto for what our enemy, Satan, does to men.

When men lack relationships with other Christian men they're more vulnerable because they're isolated. They're easier for Satan to distract, deceive, or simply demotivate when it comes to pursuing God.

Your men have buddies. They have acquaintances, pals, and amigos. What they need are friends—*real* friends—and those friends may well be waiting in your men's ministry.

Encourage friendships to form. Ways to help facilitate this include:

• **Get men talking** about more than the weather with crisp, compelling questions that prompt meaningful discussions.

• **Stay relevant** by choosing curriculum that explores what men really want to address in their lives. How will you know? You'll ask your men!

• **Share experiences.** It may be a cook-out that's rained out, a canoe trip where not one canoe stayed upright, a campfire that nobody could get started. Even "disasters" become the stuff that fuels friendships. Get men serving together and they'll find reasons to be friends.

• **Dare to go deep** with discussions that move past what men should be doing to what they're actually doing. That's where trust builds.

As you make your way through this handbook, you will discover numerous practical tools and tips to help men grow in relationship with one another.

A man at one of our meetings paused to look around the room at small groups of men leaning in, talking and praying. He then turned to me and said, "Everyone knows six people willing to carry their casket when they die. But do they have even one close friend they can call any time, day or night? It's with great thanksgiving I can now say that I do."

Because society needs godly men

This is a confusing time for men to be men.

Is it best for a man to be the strong, silent type who takes charge and leads his way through life? To be passive, disengaged and quietly fitting in? To be sensitive and caring, crying during the Hallmark movie of the week?

How can you be masculine without becoming a part of toxic masculinity—and is that even a thing?

Culture is ready and willing to define what it is to be a man. If ministries like yours don't speak into what men can and should be and how they can and should live, culture will win.

As your men's ministry looks at the life and character of Jesus, what it is to be a man takes shape. You'll encounter someone who's all-God and all-man, someone who is the very definition of what it is to be a godly man.

Why men's ministry? Because you and your ministry team keep men squarely in focus. You pray for men, connect with men, care about men. You let them lean on your shoulders when they're weak, comfort them when they're broken, pick them up and dust them off when they fall.

And you're there to celebrate the wins, too. Those moments they take a hard stand for what's right and live out priorities that reflect what God wants most for them.

Men will be quick to tell you they're doing fine on their own, and not to worry about them. But you know men well enough to not believe that.

We need the kind of men your ministry can produce. And those men need the encouragement and accountability you can provide in order to become the men they were always meant to be.

CHAPTER 2

WAYS THE BIBLE SPEAKS TO MEN'S MINISTRY

*A*s a specific ministry, the Bible doesn't address "men's ministry." Though Jesus traveled for years with a dozen men, we never see him call his crew the "Discipleship Dozen" and organize a touch football game. But that's not to say Scripture doesn't cast a vision for ministry to men. It does—because it casts a vision for who faithful men can become in Christ, what his call is on their lives, and how men can help one another grow in their faith.

Consider these passages about how, with Christ's help, men can live faithfully...

> *However, each one of you also must love his wife as he loves himself....* (Ephesians 5:33)

> *A new command I give you: Love one another. As I have loved you, so you must love one another. By this everyone will know that you are my disciples, if you love one another.* (John 13:34-35)

> *Do not let any unwholesome talk come out of your mouths, but only what is helpful for building others up according to their needs, that it may benefit those who listen. And do not grieve the Holy Spirit of God, with whom you were sealed for the day of redemption. Get rid of all bitterness, rage and anger,*

brawling and slander, along with every form of malice. Be kind and compassionate to one another, forgiving each other, just as in Christ God forgave you. (Ephesians 4:29-32)

Follow God's example, therefore, as dearly loved children and walk in the way of love, just as Christ loved us and gave himself up for us as a fragrant offering and sacrifice to God/ But among you there must not be even a hint of sexual immorality, or of any kind of impurity, or of greed, because these are improper for God's holy people. Nor should there be obscenity, foolish talk or coarse joking, which are out of place, but rather thanksgiving. (Ephesians 5:1-4)

...whoever wants to become great among you must be your servant, and whoever wants to be first must be slave of all. (Mark 10:43-45)

If you love me, keep my commands. (John 14:15)

Be alert and of sober mind. Your enemy the devil prowls around like a roaring lion looking for someone to devour. Resist him, standing firm in the faith, because you know that the family of believers throughout the world is undergoing the same kind of sufferings. (1 Peter 5:8-9)

Anyone who does not provide for their relatives, and especially for their own household, has denied the faith and is worse than an unbeliever. (1 Timothy 5:8)

But you, man of God, flee from all this, and pursue righteousness, godliness, faith, love, endurance and gentleness. (1 Timothy 6:11)

He has shown you, O mortal, what is good. And what does the Lord require of you? To act justly and to love mercy and to walk humbly with your God. (Micah 6:8)

And whatever you do, whether in word or deed, do it all in the name of the Lord Jesus, giving thanks to God the Father through him. (Colossians 3:17)

Be on your guard; stand firm in the faith; be courageous; be strong. (1 Corinthians 16:13)

Do not store up for yourselves treasures on earth, where moths and vermin destroy, and where thieves break in and steal. But store up for yourselves treasures in heaven, where moths and vermin do not destroy, and where thieves do not break in and steal. (Matthew 6:19-20)

Walk with the wise and become wise, for a companion of fools suffers harm. (Proverbs 13:20)

Two are better than one, because they have a good return for their labor: If either of them falls down, one can help the other up. But pity anyone who falls and has no one to help them up. (Ecclesiastes 4:9-10)

And how men can help one another grow…

Therefore encourage one another and build each other up, just as in fact you are doing. (1 Thessalonians 5:11)

And let us consider how we may spur one another on toward love and good deeds, not giving up meeting together, as some are in the habit of doing, but encouraging one another—and all the more as you see the Day approaching. (Hebrews 10:24-25)

Therefore confess your sins to each other and pray for each other so that you may be healed. The prayer of a righteous person is powerful and effective. (James 5:16)

As iron sharpens iron, so one person sharpens another. (Proverbs 27:17)

But wait: didn't we say these were verses for men? Aren't they verses for anyone who follows Christ, regardless of gender?

Yes. Women who follow Jesus should take these verses to heart, too. But in the context of your ministry to men these passages need to be front and center, considered and reconsidered frequently.

Ways you might do that include:

• **At meetings** you can use these as last-on-the-agenda, out-the-door commissions men hear and then carry with them as they head back into their daily lives.

• **In devotionals** you can use these verses as the basis of your thoughts, shared at ministry meetings.

• **Every so often pass around this section of the book** and have men take turns reading the passages aloud. Repetition won't guarantee the men can remember the verses word-for-word, but that's less important than their letting the passages find a place in their hearts.

CHAPTER 3

9 FOUNDATIONS OF AN EFFECTIVE MEN'S MINISTRY

*J*f you've ever built a shed, you know it's worth every hour you spend getting the foundation just right. It's a pain prepping the site, carefully checking to see that everything is perfectly level. As you lay on your belly, sighting along the ground looking for any bump or divot, you may wonder if it's really worth the effort.

It is. Make a mistake with the foundation and sooner or later your shed will be landfill. Without the right foundation nothing you build lasts. This is true with sheds, and true with your men's ministry.

It's possible the foundation for your ministry was laid long before you arrived on the scene. You might be volunteering in a ministry that's been up and running for years. Or maybe you're frantically skimming this book because your ministry's first meeting is in 30 minutes.

Either way, it never hurts to saunter around looking for any cracks in your ministry's foundation, making sure everything is sturdy and ship-shape.

Nine Non-Negotiables

There are aspects of any men's ministry that are non-negotiable. They've simply got to be in place for the ministry to draw men closer to God and encourage supportive friendships between the men.

Most are discussed in greater detail later in this book, but here's a quick list. If any are missing from your ministry, sit with your ministry's leadership and figure out how you can get them in place, pronto.

Your Ministry is Jesus-Centered

If Jesus isn't the center of your men's ministry, then what or who is? It's unfortunate, but in some ministries the social aspect takes center stage. Participants seldom talk deeply about Jesus and there doesn't seem to be any spiritual growth evidenced in men who are involved.

Here's how to tell if your ministry is Christ-Centered:

• **Jesus is elevated and praised.** You regularly take part in praising Jesus through songs, testimony, or in other ways. However it's expressed, a worshipful focus on Jesus is part of your ministry's DNA.

• **Jesus is part of the conversation.** The men in your group are learning about Jesus and discussing their discoveries with one another, their families, and those in their spheres of influence. Your men are inviting other men to come see what Jesus is doing in your men's ministry. Jesus comes up in conversation—a lot.

• **Jesus is transforming your men.** Men in your group are being transformed by the gospel and the freedom they've found in a relationship with Jesus. It shows in the way they treat each other, their wives, and their families. It shows in their involvement in ministry at your church.

In what ways is your ministry Jesus-centered? How might it become more so?

Your Ministry is Powered by Prayer

The gospels consistently show Jesus praying. He prayed among hypocrites in the temple, in crowds, on hillsides cluttered with disciples, in a crowded upper room, and frequently alone on the mountains outside Jerusalem. Many times he spent the entire night praying.

Some men in your ministry may struggle with prayer—it doesn't come naturally to them. That's especially true if you expect them to pray aloud. You'll find a stack of ideas for incorporating prayer into your ministry in Chapter 8, but here are three ways you'll be instrumental in giving prayer its proper place.

• **You'll model prayer.** As a volunteer in your ministry, you have influence—men are looking at you. Talk about prayer, teach about prayer, and most of all: pray both in ministry meetings and in your private life. Embrace regular, sincere prayer.

• **You'll help men be intercessors.** When men pray for their families, they're able to see in real time how God answers their prayers. Nothing will help men discover the power of prayer like seeing God answer in power.

• **You'll encourage men to pray.** In public, in private, anywhere and anytime—that's where you'll help your men pray as your ministry helps them learn to rely on God.

Before encouraging men in your ministry to pray, how would you describe your own prayer life? Vibrant? Dormant? Somewhere in between?

Your Ministry is Bible-Focused

Healthy men's ministries set a goal to see more men reading, studying, and obeying God's Word. Men have a hunger to know what the Bible can teach them.

Create opportunities for your men to discover how the Bible speaks into their deepest questions and concerns. Ultimately, you want to see men relating scriptural principles to themselves, their families, their work—every aspect of their lives.

Chapter 9 provides ideas for firing up your men's enthusiasm for God's Word.

Yours, too.

Your Ministry has a Clear Vision and Mission

Without these, your ministry will eventually wobble, losing focus and wander off into the woods. Vision and mission are the road map that sets your course and makes decisions easier.

If your ministry has vision and mission statements, that's great. They'll help you know where you're going. But if your leaders skipped this step and instead jumped right into Bible studies, barbeques, and baseball games, you should hit "pause" and work on those statements. If you lack vision for where you want to be in the future, you could end up anywhere. And without a mission statement you have no clarity about your objectives or how to reach them.

You'll be tempted to Google "ministry vision statement" and "ministry mission statement," adjust a few words, and claim the statements for your own.

Don't do it.

Your ministry is unique, and the process of prayerfully working out what God intends for your group is important to experience. The process helps you practice listening to God. It helps your men sharpen one another as they work together. It's a valuable, sometimes messy, process worth its weight in gold.

Your Ministry Is Intentional about Discipleship

Discipleship is how God partners with us in building his kingdom. And given that Jesus' last on-earth exhortation to his followers was to tell others about him, making disciples clearly isn't optional.

Yet some men's ministries are, for all purposes, closed groups. There's no outward focused evangelism and men don't invite friends to participate in the ministry. You seldom or never see new faces. Plus, there's little willingness to help group members grow in obedience to Christ. If a man is living in a way that's incompatible with Scripture, nobody mentions it. There's no iron-sharpening-iron happening; everyone is simply rusting away.

In your ministry do you see men growing closer to Christ? Maybe they're meeting him for the first time or deepening a relationship of 40 years. Whatever their relationship status, is it growing deeper?

Your Ministry Values Transparency and Accountability

Both are needed if you hope to see men trust one another enough to be open and honest.

Chapter 16 dives into how to build transparency and accountability, but to set the stage here are a few things you can do with your men starting today:

• **Create a Covenant of Confidentiality.** Set an expectation—one you repeat often—that what's said in your ministry meetings stays there. Create a document that says so and have men sign it. You will find a sample covenant in Chapter 16.

• **Establish small groups.** One of the best environments for your men to get to know each other and thereby begin to trust each other, is within the small group time. As men demonstrate confidentiality by keeping what is discussed only within the group, other men will feel more confident to open up about their own struggles.

• **Live it.** You can open the door to accountability relationships by being vulnerable yourself. Sharing current struggles gives permission to other men to speak more freely about what they're facing.

Your Ministry Builds Relationships

Relationships with other godly men is how men grow. And a growing relationship with Jesus is the ultimate goal of an effective men's ministry.

Does your ministry prioritize relationship building? Are there shared meals, opportunities to pray together, discussions in small groups? The most effective ministries carry the relationships beyond meeting times. Men get together to work out, grab a sandwich at a favorite deli, just do life together.

How much of that do you see happening?

Your Ministry is Service-Oriented

God calls (make that *commands*) us to love others through service. Getting men engaged in service to God and others provides purpose, proclaims Jesus, and makes for relationship building. Are the men in your ministry involved in service? What opportunities is your ministry providing for service to happen? (You'll find a list of dozens of different ways men can serve together in Chapter 17.)

Your Ministry is Moving Forward

Once men's ministries stall in place, they begin sliding backwards. That's also true of volunteers like you.

• **Are you investing in training?** There may not be a formal training or mentoring program that will enhance your ministry skills, but you can easily find online training videos to help you become a better listener, become more organized, deepen your understanding of scripture. Invest time in sharpening your skills.

• **Are you trying new things?** If you've never had a retreat or built a wheelchair ramp for an elderly neighbor, give them a try. Look for how to meet your mission in new ways. Ask God for insights as to what will bless your men and fuel their passion for him.

• **Are your men better able to apply biblical principles?** You'll know when you ask—and when you follow up from week to week, month to month. You're moving forward not just when more men show up—you could accomplish that simply by hiring the local team's pro quarterback to do an inspirational talk.

Real movement looks like men growing in Christ, and that growth is usually gradual. You have to look for it.

So, look. What do you see?

THE ANATOMY OF AN EFFECTIVE MEN'S MINISTRY

CHAPTER 4

11 QUALITIES OF EFFECTIVE MEN'S MINISTRY VOLUNTEERS

*J*ack was the second-string forward on a so-so high school basketball team whose bad fortune included being in the same league—the same *city*—as the defending state championship team.

"We had to play those guys twice during the regular season," remembers Jack, "And we knew we had zero hope of winning."

During one game Jack was called off the bench and told to contain an opposing all-state player during a man-on-man matchup.

Jack told the coach that unless he could use a bazooka, that wasn't going to happen. "I told him I wasn't as fast, I couldn't handle the ball like All-State over there, I'd never be able to block him out. I had a list of reasons I was the wrong guy for the job."

The coach held up a hand to silence Jack.

"He said this was *my* time, *my* moment; that I needed to dig deep and bring what only *I* could bring to the court.

"When I asked the coach what that was he said, 'Maybe you could cry and he'll feel sorry for you.'"

Hmmm, a little lacking as a motivational speech, but there's truth there: you can only bring what you've got to bring.

Here's good news for you as a men's ministry volunteer: You bring qualities and skills to your role. And what you don't yet have God can give you. You're a work in progress just like the men in your ministry.

The following are things that will make you especially effective in your ministry role. If they describe you—great. Thank God for them. If they don't yet describe you, ask God to help you grow in them as he transforms you into the man he knows you can be.

You're a believer

Anyone can organize meetings but if you want to do ministry—to love others as Jesus loves them—you've got to know Jesus and know him well. He's the one who fuels the insight, compassion, and love that will make you effective in ministry.

As a ministry volunteer your spiritual condition matters. You're dealing with men who are often afraid of admitting any weakness, so they're perpetually hiding who they are. They need hope and you can't give it to them if you don't have the hope of Christ in your own heart.

So ask yourself: Is your friendship with Jesus growing, going, or somewhere in between? How are you tending to your friendship with Jesus?

You're a person of prayer

You're not in this ministry thing alone, you know.

If Jesus has called you into this he's looking to encourage and equip you along the way. He's your partner in this endeavor and partners need to stay connected. One way is to pray—frequently and honestly.

"Frequently" and "honestly." How well do those words describe your prayer life?

You know the Bible

No, you don't need to memorize the whole thing. But you do need to know the story laid out in Scripture: How people seem determined to sin and how God has responded with love, paving a road home to himself through the death and resurrection of Jesus.

And it's good to know portions of the Bible that speak to issues commonly faced by men. See Chapter 23 for a cheat sheet of passages you'll want to know.

You show empathy

Let's just say it: There are some men who equate showing emotion with weakness. They don't want talk about their feelings even if their feelings are eating them alive. If that describes you, you're going to have a difficult time helping hurting men, Here's the unvarnished truth: *all* men are hurting men. Whether or not you can see it, they're *all* wounded, and Jesus wants to heal those wounds, maybe through you and your ministry.

So get comfortable owning your feelings and giving others permission to feel what they're feeling. It's okay. Really. Feelings don't give you cancer.

And here's a hint: If a man seems angry and there doesn't seem to be any reasonable explanation for that anger, it might be he's really feeling hurt, or betrayed, or like a failure. All sorts of feelings come bursting out of some men looking like anger.

You're courageous

It takes courage to sit with a man and tell him he needs to repent of a sin. To walk alongside a man who's hurting. To share something painful you're going through to make the room safe for other men to do the same.

That courage comes from Christ and a deep love for the men you serve.

You keep first things first

Your goal is to bring men deeper into a friendship with Jesus.

Don't let that message get lost as you create a schedule of programs and activities. Day trips to the art museum are wonderful, but unless you make a spiritual connection you've wasted the day.

Always be asking Jesus, "What do you want to make of this moment?"

You set boundaries

Your ministry leader can help you here, so ask about it.

As a trusted person in the lives of men you can expect some 2:00 a.m. phone calls when a man's wife has left him, his son has been in a car accident, he's lost a job, or found a tumor.

Are you willing to take those calls?

You're called to serve, but somewhere there's an outer limit of what you can deliver. And you don't want to make a promise you can't or won't keep.

Decide on your boundaries now, before you're forced to do so on the spot. Ask Jesus where he'd set them and then serve joyfully within them.

You can live with silence

Sometimes a man doesn't want to talk about it. Period.

Are you okay just sitting with a man you serve and not giving advice he doesn't want, not sharing a scripture that he's not ready to hear?

Sometimes showing up is all that's wanted and more than enough.

You're humble and teachable

This ministry will humble you in a heartbeat. Just about the time you think you've got your men figured out you discover that the guy you wrote off as a perpetual grump actually has four herniated discs and has been pain every day for three years. Your assumption was wrong—and it's not your only assumption that's wrong.

Can you admit you're imperfect? That you've got a lot to learn? If not, you're tripping over your pride and that won't serve you well in ministry.

Ask Jesus to ease you into humility. It may save you having him dump you into the deep end of the humility pool.

You make room for more male friendships

Men's ministry isn't something you do from a distance. Do you have the bandwidth to add some new friends to your circle?

You're willing to get enough sleep to be effective

You're likely a busy guy. Work, home, church, you've got a lot of plates to keep spinning.

Which makes it tempting to cut short sleep and exercise so you can get stuff done, and that's a mistake. You need to develop the skill of getting enough sleep because serving in this ministry can be demanding. There's prep work to do before meetings, follow-up conversations to have, and calls to take when men are struggling.

So get some sleep. Really. Going into men's meetings rested allows you to stay sharp, noticing what's said and who said it, hearing the meaning behind the words. Rest gives you the ability to do better, deeper ministry.

No more midnight movie marathons for you, at least the day before a ministry meeting.

Men's Ministry Roles

If you're reading this book, chances are you are either already a part of the men's ministry team at your church or considering plugging into a role on the team. Whether a part of a new or existing ministry, some roles to pray about serving in or consider incorporating include:

Director: In very large churches, this might be a staff position, but in many churches it's not uncommon for a ministry to be led by a volunteer. If you're in this role, be it as staff or volunteer, be mindful to not try and do everything yourself. The ministry and the men you serve will benefit from a strong team.

Small Group Leader: Any healthy and growing men's ministry has a continuous need to train and raise up group leaders. Often there are misconceptions about what makes a good small group leader. Practically speaking, more important than being a great teacher or Bible scholar, an effective group leader *facilitates* a meeting well. Someone who is able to keep things on track, ask good questions, and listen well.

Events and/or Service Coordinator: If the men's ministry at your church has a vision for putting on special events for men, having someone with the skills and abilities to help organize and keep up with the details may be just what the team needs. Likewise, if the ministry you are a part of wants to major on having men make an impact through service, having someone focused on identifying and organizing service opportunities can be invaluable.

Communications and/or Prayer Coordinator: It's hard to overstate the importance of good communication. Having someone who not only knows how to relay pertinent information in a timely manner, but also knows who to contact and the best way to reach them can be a real difference maker. If there's a particular focus on prayer in your men's ministry, you might have or want to consider a point person or small team dedicated to helping facilitate and lead prayer and prayer events.

No two men's ministries are exactly alike. Regardless of your role on the team, knowing and applying the qualities covered in this chapter will help you and the ministry thrive!

CHAPTER 5

6 BEST PRACTICES IN MEN'S MINISTRY

*H*ere's something you may not know about me: I helped found a men's ministry in Florida. What started as several men meeting in a home grew into a multi-campus organization ministering to hundreds of men in the Tampa Bay area and beyond.

We didn't intend to create a ministry of that size. There wasn't some grand plan; we just kept inviting friends to something that was changing lives—ours included.

During the early years of our *Wildmen* ministry we had to stretch, solve problems, brainstorm solutions, experiment, and sometimes claw our way through the zillion challenges that come with growing a ministry. And prayers—boy, did we pray.

Along the way we learned what works in men's ministry and what doesn't. And I'm grateful that in this book I can share with you what we discovered as well as what other ministry workers have found to be true.

We're helping you avoid making the mistakes we made, so you're welcome.

And we're also sharing with you best practices—key elements that can help you in your ministry. If you're already implementing them, you're ahead of the game.

But if you haven't, consider the following six things:

Offer Small Groups

Our ministry started as a small group, and we wanted every man to experience that sense of connection and accountability we were enjoying—so we invited guys. Lots of guys.

You can guess what happened.

Our small group quickly became a large group, and it was more and more difficult to maintain a small group feel. We realized when once you get to eight guys in a group that's as large as you can grow before group dynamics suffer.

So we formed "platoons." That's just another word for "small groups," but doesn't it sound manlier?

At our meetings we'd eat together, sing a few (man-appropriate) worship songs, watch a video study or hear from a speaker, then split up into platoons.

That large group/small group format allowed us to both enjoy the whole group of guys and also have smaller groups where men could ask questions, share concerns, and pray for one another as they built relationships.

We considered platoon time the most important element of the meeting because that's where the real, rubber-meets-the-road ministry happened.

Chapters 14 and 15 will deal more deeply with how to build relationships in a small group setting, but for now just make this best practice note: *you need small groups.*

Be a Safe Place

Men have to trust each other to be open and honest. Without trust, your men will never develop much-needed accountability relationships. Without being a safe place where men can be themselves and ask hard questions, you may as well go back to those pancake breakfasts.

Becoming a safe place won't happen until men believe that what happens at men's ministry will stay at men's ministry.

Which—to be honest—you can't promise.

You can't guarantee some guy won't post on social media what was revealed in his small group. You can't guarantee that someone won't say something you're compelled to pass along to your ministry leader or pastor.

But you can set an expectation of confidentiality and do specific things to make that part of your culture. You'll find specifics in Chapter 16.

Serve Food

From the start our men's ministry provided a meal for everyone present. I won't lie: It's not easy to plan, shop for, prepare, serve, and clean up after a bunch of hungry (and sometimes picky) men.

But many of our guys came directly from work and arrived hungry and in need of time to decompress. We saw relationships form as guys ate together. My friend and co-leader, Jan, pointed out that sharing a meal dropped the barriers men carried in with them, which meant men were far more likely to receive what the Lord had for them.

Jan was right.

Maybe you've got guys who love to cook. If so, set them free to form a team that prepares meals for meetings. Or cater the meals and save both time and effort.

If budget is an issue (and isn't it always) do what we did and put a basket at the beginning of the buffet. We asked men to donate what they could so we could continue providing meals. We also mentioned there was no obligation to donate. Many times the money in the basket more than paid for the food.

If your ministry is small or you simply can't handle serving a meal, the "serve food" best practice still holds: place a few bowls of chips in the meeting room.

Maybe it's not your call about providing food. Maybe you meet at a time when there's no need for a full meal.

But you can't go wrong with those bowls of chips. Trust me.

Over-Communicate

Communicate to your men as often and in as many ways you can. Guys are busy and some haven't updated their calendars since 2004.

Here are ways to keep ministry meetings and events in front of your men...

• **Worship service announcements.** On screen, in the bulletin, mentioned from the pulpit—they all work. And if your men are in the service, they'll hear that reminder.

• **Send emails.** You collected your guys' contact information, right? Use it.

• **Send texts.** Not everyone reads emails.

• **Call your guys.** They may not answer but they'll have voice mail.

• **Tell their wives.** Not recommended as a strategy, but *highly* effective.

Communicating often works wonders when it comes to getting men to special events or even to weekly meetings. Your efforts reinforce they're welcome, that the meetings are valuable, and that they're on your radar.

Meet Frequently

Some men's ministries meet bi-weekly or even monthly. If that's the existing tempo of your meetings there's probably a good reason that schedule was set.

But be aware that the longer the time between meetings, the more difficult it is to maintain momentum with your men. The harder it is for them to form friendships. The more challenging it is to be present in one another's lives.

Yes, it's a lot of work to facilitate a meeting weekly rather than once a month. But if you're meeting less than weekly, would you and the leaders of your ministry prayerfully consider finding a way to connect more often with the men you serve?

The benefits are powerful.

Add Worship—and Singing

I remember like it was yesterday:

I'd only met with the guys who formed the nucleus of *Wildmen* for a few weeks. But each of those weeks I longingly walked past a beautiful grand piano on my way to the kitchen. So one week I said, "Hey, I noticed that piano. Would you be interested in adding a few worship songs to our meeting each week?"

Crickets.

After a few awkward moments, one of the men said, "Let me get this straight: You want a bunch of men to stand around a piano *singing songs?*"

The next week, I printed up lyric sheets to songs I figured they already knew plus a few simple songs that weren't hard to pick up. And, maybe just to humor me, they trudged on out to the piano and gave singing together a try.

From that day forward, a few worship songs before the teaching has been an important part of our weekly meetings. There's something about men singing together that bonds them as they turn their attention to God. It gives me chills.

But if you're going to sing in your ministry, you've got to do it right. Otherwise what can be a best practice can quickly become a disaster.

Here's how to get your guys singing:

• **Pick familiar songs** that are also easy to sing.

• **Provide lyric sheets or project the lyrics on a screen** so men who don't know the songs won't feel awkward. Also, the "I didn't know the song" excuse for not joining in evaporates.

- **Choose a "man friendly" key.** No notes that require a step ladder to hit.

- **If you don't have skilled musicians, sing along with recorded songs.** But here's a caution: avoid songs recorded by women.

- **If you're bringing in a musician, make it a man.** Men who aren't confident about their voices get all weird when singing in front of a woman. No, I don't know why.

- **Avoid songs with fluffy or romantic lyrics.** As a worship leader, I'd love if the men at our meetings were so in love with Jesus that they could boldly sing it out loud and proud. But not everyone at my meetings—or your meetings—is at that place. So pick songs with themes about conquering, victory, adventure, the holiness of God, our God and King, and the like.

- **Keep it short and sweet.** Unless the Holy Spirit says otherwise, a couple songs and wrap it up. And don't try to force intimate worship moments.

Remember: *you aren't obligated to sing*. Worship music may not be a good fit for your group. If that's the case, no worries. There are plenty of other ways to worship God.

SECTION 3

MEN'S MINISTRY IDEAS, TIPS, AND TOOLS

CHAPTER 6

DEALING WITH PORN
(THE ELEPHANT IN THE ROOM)

The fact men struggle with sexual sin and porn is probably no surprise.

When the author of the website *Communicate Jesus* surveyed men and asked, "What is the number one sin you would like to put to death in your life?" 60% of men under 45 years named sexual sin.

And those are just the ones being honest.

With mobile devices and Internet, men are exposed to pornography far younger than ever. According to Covenant Eyes, 64% of Christian men say they view pornography at least once a month, with pornography being the topic of 20% of all searches on mobile devices.

Victims of this prevalent struggle include families, marriages, and ministries. And let's not forget about participants in the sex industry, who often find themselves trapped by sex traffickers or financial promises that never come to fruition.

What Should Your Ministry Do?

There's a great need for men (and boys) to be equipped to deal with sexual temptation. So, discuss with your ministry leaders and church leaders whether your ministry will deal with this issue or not.

Wait. I know what you're thinking: "I thought you said a majority of men struggle with sexual sin. Shouldn't the men's ministry be *the* place to deal with it?"

Yes. And no.

If your team includes men who are trained to help in this area, then yes, your ministry might want to consider a plan. If not, it may be best to refer men to professionals when they make you aware of their struggle.

If you decide to deal with it but could use training, there are resources available to help you get going. You will find one of these listed below, and additional resources listed in Chapter 25. Whatever you decide, it's important for you and other ministry volunteers to know your group's protocol.

It's easy to treat pornography as an item on a checklist that gets addressed once in a while. Unfortunately, simply sharing what the Bible says regarding sexual purity won't win this battle.

In the early days of our men's ministry we chose not to deal with this issue as a whole group. Instead, when leadership became aware of a situation, that man was assisted individually and with great care and confidentiality.

Healing and restoration was always the goal.

It wasn't an easy decision. I remember many leadership meetings discussing how we could create some kind of separate, anonymous small group designed to confront the issue head on. But who would lead it? What curriculum would we use? And how could we advertise this group to our men while still keeping it anonymous? And would men, who work hard to keep their pornography use secret, be willing to step forward and meet with other men?

After several failed attempts over the years, one group of men came to leadership and offered to run such a small group. A group was formed that met separately over the next 16-weeks.

Reports were that God was dealing with the men and they were seeing breakthroughs. Even after that specific study concluded, that group continued to meet as an accountability group.

I'm not suggesting you switch directions if your ministry has another approach to dealing with sexual sin. And I'm not 100% sure our group handled it in the best way possible. Do what God is telling you to do.

I'm just cautioning you that porn addiction can be more difficult to deal with than other areas of sin. It's like drug or alcohol addiction because there are biochemical factors involved that drive the brain to want more and more.

But don't let this issue—which is almost certainly impacting men in your group—arise without your having decided how you'll address it. Discuss the issue now so you're ready to respond.

Train the Trainer

Perhaps a good place to start is to have ministry leaders, and volunteers like you, go through training about how to deal with pornography. At the time of this printing, one option is the "Pornography Education Course for Church Leaders," available from Covenant Eyes. There's a nominal cost, and the license is for your entire organization. You can find out more on their website.[3]

Covenant Eyes also offers pastors and ministry leaders free one-hour seminars. Search their site for information about their Pastor Roundtables or sign up for their Monthly Pastor's Newsletter.

Again: Act Now

With the pervasiveness of pornography, you can safely assume it's impacting men within the ministry you serve. There's damage being done to those men, to their families, to their spiritual lives.

Were a rabid dog running around your meetings, occasionally taking a bite from the shin of a man, you'd slam on the brakes and deal with the dog before anyone else was hurt.

Well, there's a rabid dog and it's porn.

Whatever you decide to do, do it now.

---

3   https://covenant-eyes-communities.teachable.com/p/porn-
     education-ministry-staff-conversations-covenant-eyes

CHAPTER 7

COPING WITH CURRICULUM

*W*ith any men's ministry one of the immediate and ongoing challenges is figuring out what resources to utilize.

Most men's ministries decide to pick a curriculum and immediately discover there are so many books and video-based options that picking one sometimes feels overwhelming.

If you're volunteering in a ministry whose leadership has selected a curriculum, you don't need to scout out a selection. But your leaders will want to know if what's being used is working—and if it's not, you'll want to offer alternatives.

In my years of weekly men's ministry, I've used group studies ranging from topical to practical to specific books of the Bible. Some proved to be top-notch, high-quality materials that would work with any group.

But some studies fell short. Most often the problem wasn't the content itself. It was that, for whatever reason, the studies simply didn't resonate with my men at that time.

Following are practical suggestions for selecting and sharing the right curriculum with your group.

• Ask men what questions they want to explore in the Bible

That wording is intentional. If you ask men what they want to *study* in the Bible you're signing them up for school. But if you ask them what *questions* they want to explore—that's a journey of discovery. It's an adventure. And the topics they select can guide curriculum selection.

• Plan ahead

Prayerfully discuss with your leaders what topics your men need to grapple with.

Sure, there are basics that work with most any group. But your group of men may have unique issues and immediate, felt needs that *must* be addressed before they'll find a general study on the book of Mark relevant to their lives.

Brainstorm what issues seem urgent and let that list guide any hunt for curriculum. And keep your eyes out for what lessons you'll use when the series you have in hand are finished. Waiting until the last minute to select curriculum is a leading cause of headaches, heartaches, and upset stomach.

Plan ahead and plan to stay ahead.

• Realize lessons may not be the most important part of your meeting

Yes, you want God's Word explored and experienced, to see men growing in their faith. And solid, Bible-based lessons help that happen.

But your men have dozens of places they can access Bible information. Books, podcasts, television shows, radio, magazines: there's an avalanche of information out there.

It may be that what your men most need are healthy relationships with other men, relationships that are honest, encouraging, and non-competitive. Which means your meetings have to balance lessons with fellowship.

Some advice: err on the side of fellowship. And if you pick the right curriculum some of that fellowship will happen during the lessons.

• Pick curriculum that's less lecture, more discussion

If you're doing all the talking at your meetings, that's probably a problem. There's a place for lectures, but a steady diet casts your men in the role of observers, not participants.

When selecting curriculum, pick lessons that include open-ended questions. Those are questions that can't be answered with a simple "yes" or "no," or by reciting a fact from the lecture. Open-ended questions pull men into discussions.

• Look for short lessons—or shorten those you find

People in general have shorter attention spans than they had a generation ago, and men are no exception.

Here's what that means to you: Be generous with the food and fellowship portion of your meeting and cut the actual lesson time a bit. Ask speakers and teachers to get their lesson's point across in 20 instead of 30-minutes.

And if you can stick with a topic for between 4 and 8-weeks, as a general rule of thumb, that's about all your men will want to hear before moving on to a new topic.

Also, post a conversation starter on the door so men see it as they enter the room. It gives shy or new men a launching pad to initiate a discussion.

Here are a few potential starters:

— Describe what life was like for you when you were twelve.
— What was your first pet's name? How did you feel about the pet?
— What was Christmas morning like when you were a child?
— What's your favorite sort of music? Why that style?
— Who's someone famous you've either met or would like to meet?
— If you could give a piece of advice to yourself back when you were a pre-teen, what would it be?
— What's a lesson you learned you'll never forget? How did you learn it?
— Your first car: What was it, how did you get it, and what became of it?

— What's a question you'd ask God if you knew you'd get a direct answer?

When it comes to lessons, here are a few things to keep in mind:

• **If you use video-based lessons, debrief what you see**

There will probably be questions provided by the curriculum provider—use them. Failing to debrief a lesson means you fail to pull meaning from the viewing experience, and miss making personal application.

When debriefing lessons you or another volunteer needs to be careful to…

• **Do not judge responses.** Doing so shuts down the conversation.

• **Remain neutral.** Especially with sensitive topics, you'll have an opinion. Keep it to yourself and instead encourage men to share theirs.

• **Make sure those who want to speak have the chance to do so.** One way to accomplish this is to have men share in pairs rather than take comments from the whole group.

• **Stay on task.** Conversations can quickly hop on down bunny trails. Intervene and keep comments relevant to the topic at hand.

• **Drive toward application.** The questions provided may or may not go there; be sure to add some if necessary. In light of what you saw, what if anything will you do?

• **Keep it fresh**

Someone should carve it in stone: Bored men are inattentive men.

So before jumping into a list of recommended curricula, let's consider how you can keep things fresh from meeting to meeting no matter what curriculum you or your leaders select. Changing things up from time to time works wonders to ward off the yawns and any hint of redundancy and cookie-cutter meetings.

• Schedule a bye week between series

Plowing straight into the next study may not always be the best approach. In place of taking the week off, you may want to consider some of the serving together suggestions in Chapter 17.

• Switch up discussion partners or groups

During discussion times consider having men shift who they're debriefing a question with. It widens perspective and also helps men connect with new people who may become fast friends.

• Vary the elements of your meeting

There's no law that says you have to end your meeting with prayer. What if you did that first? Or you cut the two songs you usually sing and substitute a sharing time? Not letting your meetings become predictable is a way to keep them fresh.

• Change the venue

Does the facility you currently meet offer any kind of outdoor space where you could meet? Maybe there's a public park nearby. What about telling your men to meet one week at the local bowling alley or restaurant?

Options for alternative meeting spaces depend on the size of your group, the weather, tech needs and other factors, but look to make a switch happen now and then.

• Pull out props

Ask creative folks on your team to brainstorm props, video clips, or other visual elements to reflect the study theme and keep things visually interesting. Not only does this help keep the men's attention, it demonstrates your leadership and volunteer team is willing to go the extra mile to make things special. For example, if you're doing a study that has the word "Building" or "Constructing" in the title, place tools on the stage or around the room to add ambiance.

Though here's a caution: Don't make props *too* interesting. Jerry owns an asphalt company and decided to highlight a "Building a Firm

Foundation" meeting theme by placing dump trucks, tractors, and pavers in the field next to his church. That way guys would have to walk past them on the way in. Except they didn't exactly walk *past* the machinery; they mostly walked *to* the machinery. It took a promise they could climb into the cabs after the meeting to get guys inside.

• Co-opt Hollywood

My friend David Dusek has a ministry called Rough Cut Men where he uses relevant clips from major motion pictures like "Saving Private Ryan," "Rudy," Armageddon," "Top Gun," and "Walk the Line" to grab men's attention and prompt conversations about lesson topics.

Check to make sure you're sticking within legal limits as to how much footage you show in a public meeting like this. Generally speaking, if you keep it short you're in good shape.

• Let them practice what you preach

How about letting your men practice *their* preaching skills? One popular study we did was on the book of James. It's a book in the New Testament with five chapters so, several weeks before the study started, we invited five men in the group to each cover one chapter.

These five men were to study their chapter and in 15 to 20 minutes present the content of the chapter using whatever technology or props they wanted.

You might think this was risky. And you'd be right. Our men did a fabulous job, prompting other men to ask if they could be involved next go 'round. But it could have gone the other way, too.

The key to success is prayerfully considering who to ask to present a lesson, and then giving those presenters plenty of time to prepare. Also, you might ask your presenters to meet with you or other leaders to review the presentations prior to sharing with the entire group.

Giving other men the chance to lead not only keeps everyone interested, it builds their investment in the group. And it keeps your meetings from becoming predictable.

And technically speaking . . .

Do whatever you need to do so men can see and hear during your meetings. Which means unless you're a small group sitting in a living room, you'll need to deal with audio and video. Not every facility is set up for video and not every men's group has someone savvy when it comes to audio and video.

It's worth the effort to either find someone in your group who's capable or watch enough YouTube how-to videos that you become proficient yourself. Free training is available.

Here's good news: the price of projectors has fallen and sometimes a laptop, HDMI cable, and low-cost projector you can aim at a blank wall is all you need to show a video clip to a room of 50 men.

In a living room a smart TV or good-sized laptop will handle the visuals, and everyone can hear the presenter just fine.

Keep this in mind: As your group grows in size, so will your A/V needs.

Video studies that work

Video studies can be very effective. I've listed some recommendations in Chapter 25. More come out constantly so keep your eyes open for new options.

CHAPTER 8

PRAYING AS A GROUP

*P*rayer. Seems so simple, right?

So why is it that so many of us do it so seldom? The Barna Group found that less than seven in 10 Americans (69%) pray weekly.[4]

Not daily—*weekly*.

And among those people who rarely pray may be some of your men.

Your Men and Prayer

If you grew up in the church, prayer may seem like a normal part of life. But how many of the men you serve grew up in a home where prayer was a regular occurrence? How many of them saw meaningful prayer modeled?

I've found at least four reasons men in ministries I've been part of fail to pray:

• **A lack of focus.** You're settling in to talk with God about life and then you remember: There's a report due at work. Your wife's birthday is tomorrow. You forgot to clean out the gutters. It's hard to talk about life when life gets in the way.

• **A lack of discipline.** Of course we should pray. But we should also jog two miles a day and is that happening? Self-discipline is seldom our drug of choice.

---

4   https://www.barna.com/research/changing-state-of-the-church

• **The enemy loves to run interference.** Since the prayer of a righteous man can accomplish much (see James 5:16), Satan doesn't want your men praying. He's not eager to see the power that will unleash.

Oh, and there's a fourth reason, too:

• **Many men don't understand prayer.** If God already knows everything, why tell him stuff? What exactly are you supposed to say and do when you pray? If you get prayer wrong, how much trouble are you in with God?

One way you can benefit the men in your ministry is to help them understand and then experience the power of consistent, fervent prayer in their lives.

Here's how to do just that.

First, share what Jesus said about prayer

Jesus presents short course on prayer in his Sermon on the Mount. Show your men the three points Jesus made in Matthew 6:5-13:

1. Pray privately. (See Matthew 6:5,6)
2. Pray humbly and reverently. (See Matthew 6:7,8)
3. Pray as Jesus prayed. (See the Lord's prayer in Matthew 6:9-13)

With that background, help men experience dynamic, purposeful prayer that's specific and active. Without veering into a Bible study on prayer, let me point out seven types of prayer found in the Bible and suggest how they might look in the context of your men's ministry.

Prayers of Intercession

In 1 Timothy 2:1, we read, "I urge, then, first of all, that petitions, prayers, intercession and thanksgiving be made for all people…"

Intercession is prayer that pleads with God for your needs and the needs of others.

How might it impact your men if they stood outside city hall in your town and together prayed for those who serve inside to have wisdom in making decisions? Not to advocate for one policy or another, but that God's will be done?

Prayers of Faith

James tells us in James 5:15, "… the prayer offered in faith will make the sick person well; the Lord will raise them up. If they have sinned, they will be forgiven."

Prayers of faith ask God to accomplish what he's promised in his Word.

After your men meet early some morning as the sun rises to pray that Jesus returns soon they'll never see another sunrise without remembering that prayer, and God's promise.

Prayers of Agreement

You might call this corporate prayer. Jesus talks about the power of corporate prayer in Matthew 18:19 when he says, "Again, truly I tell you that if two of you on earth agree about anything they ask for, it will be done for them by my Father in heaven."

What can your men agree to pray about? What are they willing to trust God to do?

Prayers of Thanksgiving

Psalm 95:2-3 says, "Let us come before him with thanksgiving and extol him with music and song. For the Lord is the great God, the great King above all gods."

If your men are like most believers they're big on asking, less good at saying "thank you."

Challenge your guys to pray as a group for a full ten minutes without asking for anything. Instead, the prayer will be pure gratitude.

Prayers of Worship

David was one for worship prayers. Consider the opening of Psalm 63: "You, God, are my God, earnestly I seek you; I thirst for you, my whole being longs for you, in a dry and parched land where there is no water."

Pick a blistering summer day and invite your men on a hike out into the middle of nowhere. When they're ready to drop, share this passage and bottled water; your men will make a connection that sticks.

Prayers of Request

Paul tells us in Philippians 4:6, "Do not be anxious about anything, but in every situation, by prayer and petition, with thanksgiving, present your requests to God."

God wants to hear from us when we need something for ourselves or others. Those prayers are vivid reminders that God is the source of blessings, that we depend on him.

Encourage your men to pray for themselves but make a regular practice of pairing men up and having them pray for their partners, too.

Prayers of Consecration

Romans 12:1 says, "Therefore, I urge you, brothers and sisters, in view of God's mercy, to offer your bodies as a living sacrifice, holy and pleasing to God—this is your true and proper worship."

Paul is urging us to dedicate our bodies to God's service. That's not a bad thing for you to have your men do, too, by perhaps inking a dot on an inside wrist as a reminder. When our physical bodies are set aside for God's use, there's a whole lot of sinning we won't be able to do.

Notice that none of these approaches to prayer have your men sitting quietly with heads bowed and eyes closed. To be clear: there's nothing wrong with that traditional approach to prayer—but it's not a biblical mandate. And your men's prayers will be far more engaged and active if *they're* active in some way.

That's how most of us guys are wired.

Incorporating prayer into your men's ministry

There are logical places prayer fits into the flow of your ministry. If you're already taking advantage of them, great. If not, how can you slide prayer into these connection points?

• **Encourage leaders to pray before meetings.** In your volunteer role you may or may not show up early at meetings to huddle with other volunteers and leaders. If you do, ask that the men there pray for each other, the guys coming to the meeting, your church, and your pastors.

• **Open meetings with prayer.** Invite different men to offer these prayers, but don't spring the request on them. Ask them prior to the meeting.

• **Have small group leaders open and close with prayer.** Small group leaders are the volunteers who hear the real needs of men and can facilitate prayers that are personal and specific. Small group leaders can also remind their men to keep praying by sending out that week's prayer requests, *IF* the men making requests give permission to have those requests shared. Remember: confidentiality includes prayer requests, too.

• **Share answered prayers with the larger group.** Nothing prompts heartfelt praise like hearing how God is answering prayer. And what an encouragement for others to pray, too.

• **Consider forming a prayer team consisting of known prayer warriors.** Ask the guys who are drawn to pray to come to meetings a few minutes early and pray over every seat in which a man will be seated. Consider asking prayer warriors not in your group to pray throughout ministry meetings. Provide those warriors a curated list of prayer requests that arose during the meetings.

• **Host an occasional men's prayer night.** The church worship team can kick things off with a few songs inviting the Holy Spirit to be present and then a leader can lead men in voicing prayers for your ministry, your church, your community, your nation, and world events.

• **Provide a prayer box in your meeting area.** Men who aren't comfortable talking about their prayer needs can fill out requests, knowing that someone will pray for them.

• **Partner with another men's ministry and pray for one another.** How great to read aloud a letter from a group of men across the nation letting your men know those distant brothers are praying for them?

And if you should happen to have a retreat:

Okay, I'm going to call your retreat an "advance" or "boot camp" because I just *hate* the word "retreat" in the context of men's ministry. Bear with me—and consider banishing the word "retreat" from your event vocabulary, too.

If you host an *advance*, here's how to power up the event with prayer:

• **Sign up people to pray for each man who'll be attending.** You can even have people for "slots" on the registration list that don't yet have names in them.

• **Go 24/7 with prayer.** Ask people to pray throughout the event by having them sign up to pray in half-hour increments. Let your men know that at 2:30 a.m. someone was asking God to bless them; that knowledge will humble your men.

• **Put up a prayer "tent."** It's an area men can go at any time during the event to ask for prayer. Have someone in the tent at all times during the event, day and night.

• **Ask families to pray for their men.** If possible, get a letter from a spouse or child that lets men know they're being lifted up in prayer. You'll see men weep when opening those letters during your event; they'll know they're loved and bathed in prayer.

CHAPTER 9

GROUNDING MEN IN SCRIPTURE

*T*o let Scripture speak into their lives, your guys need to spend time with the Bible.

As in *reading* the Bible, which, based on research from the Barna Group, appears to be a fading art form.[5]

It's likely that a significant number of men in your church have little or no input from Scripture apart from what they get at worship services or your ministry meetings. For decades Bible reading has trended steadily downward. All along that downward slope men have consistently been less likely than women to engage in Bible reading. It's been like that for decades so, if you want your men to open their Bibles more faithfully, something has to happen.

And that something is you.

You and other ministry volunteers can show men the value of being grounded in Scripture. You won't accomplish that by shaming men for not reading Scripture or attempting to guilt them into daily devotions.

Instead, take a tip from the marketing community and highlight the benefits of Bible reading. Tell your men what's in it for them.

Consider these benefits below:

---

5   Barna: State of the Bible 2021 (https://www.barna.com/research/sotb-2021)

MEN'S MINISTRY VOLUNTEER HANDBOOK

• Reading the Bible reveals God's character

The Bible tells God's story. Your men will discover who he is as they watch him interact with his creation, hear what he says about himself, and see what he reveals through Jesus.

Following are just a few passages that pull back the curtain and let your men catch a glimpse of God:

> *The Lord is not slow in keeping his promise, as some understand slowness. Instead he is patient with you, not wanting anyone to perish, but everyone to come to repentance.* (2 Peter 3:9)

> *This is the message we have heard from him and declare to you: God is light; in him there is no darkness at all.* (1 John 1:5)

> *Do you not know? Have you not heard? The Lord is the everlasting God, the Creator of the ends of the earth. He will not grow tired or weary, and his understanding no one can fathom.* (Isaiah 40:28)

Asking your men what these—and many more—passages tell them about God launches deep conversations that teach your men to come to the Bible not just for good advice and moral instruction, but to meet its author: God himself.

• Reading the Bible helps keep men from sinning

It's easy for your men to do the wrong thing if they don't know what the right thing is. The Bible sheds describes the actions and attitudes that please God.

When writing about how young people could be pure, the author of Psalm 119 included this passage in his advice:

I have hidden your word in my heart that I might not sin against you. (Psalm 119:11)

When God's Word sinks deeply into men's hearts and minds, it installs an alarm that sounds when their behavior strays away from God and toward sin. The truth they've learned protects them.

Encourage your men to read the Bible because it lights the path to God-pleasing behavior. It helps them not to disobey or disappoint the God they love.

• Reading the Bible helps your men grow up spiritually

When men come to know, love, and abide in Jesus, they grow spiritually. The Apostle Paul describes what happens then in a letter to Christians in Ephesus:

Then we will no longer be infants, tossed back and forth by the waves, and blown here and there by every wind of teaching and by the cunning and craftiness of people in their deceitful scheming. Instead, speaking the truth in love, we will grow to become in every respect the mature body of him who is the head, that is, Christ. (Ephesians 4:14-15)

Men can get older without growing up—just ask their wives. When men are in God's Word, actively letting it shape them, they not only grow older, they mature spiritually.

• Reading the Bible gives your men courage and strength

Both are required to stand for Christ and walk faithfully with him. The Bible introduces your men to faithful believers and helps them discover what fueled those saints' courage and strength...

I can do all this through him who gives me strength.
(Philippians 4:13)

God is our refuge and strength, an ever-present help in trouble. (Psalm 46:1)

Bible reading builds your men's faith and gives them courage and strength.

• Reading the Bible renews your men's minds

Half the challenges men face as followers of Jesus would disappear were they to discipline their thought life.

The Bible helps that happen:

Finally, brothers and sisters, whatever is true, whatever is noble, whatever is right, whatever is pure, whatever is lovely, whatever is admirable—if anything is excellent or praiseworthy—think about such things. (Philippians 4:8)

Do not conform to the pattern of this world, but be transformed by the renewing of your mind. Then you will be able to test and approve what God's will is—his good, pleasing and perfect will. (Romans 12:2)

As your men read Scripture, it reads them in return. It seeks and speaks into the places where transformation is needed.

• Reading the Bible gives your men hope

Life can be discouraging, but life in Christ never is—so encourage your men to spend time with him in the Bible. Once your men grasp that nothing can pull them from the safety of God's love, and that there's hope in him, life has a fresh perspective.

…but those who hope in the LORD will renew their strength. They will soar on wings like eagles; they will run and not grow weary, they will walk and not be faint. (Isaiah 40:31)

For I am convinced that neither death nor life, neither angels nor demons, neither the present nor the future, nor any powers, neither height nor depth, nor anything else in all creation, will be able to separate us from the love of God that is in Christ Jesus our Lord. (Romans 8:38-39)

Minus a steady diet of Scripture your men's spiritual growth is stunted. So you and your ministry need to get more Bible reading on the menu.

But how?

Early on in men's ministry I realized I wasn't the only one struggling to carve out time to read the Bible. So I challenged a group of men to read one chapter of the Bible each day—beginning with Hebrews.

After completing a chapter, men sent an email to the group saying it was done and sharing any insights that came to them.

I was amazed by what I read. Not only did I gain insights from my own reading, but I also learned much from the insights of the other men.

Fast forward four years and, with a few exceptions, we were all still reading Scripture and emailing one another. Our lives were transformed by this simple practice, and it wasn't just our lives that were changed. One of the guys in our ministry decided to do the same thing with his family. He'd struggled to get his four teenage daughters together to discuss the Bible but sending emails? They were in.

As were the families of some of their friends. And a local youth group. And the entire church that youth group visited on a mission project. I was thrilled to find out dozens of groups were using this simple accountability model to encourage Bible reading.

More and more men in our ministry were picking up their Bibles, but they weren't quite sure how to approach reading them.

So I came up with an acronym to help them engage with Scripture: PROMPT. It's an easy, six-step approach that helps men encounter God in their reading.

And I'm officially deputizing you to use this technique with your men, too.

P – Pray. Before reading the Bible ask God to help you focus and hear what he has for you. Invite the Holy Spirit to help you understand what you're reading.

R – Read. Engage with the text, reading thoughtfully.

O – Observe. What's happening in the text you're reading? Who's speaking? Who's the audience? It's important to understand these details to get the big picture.

M – Meditate. God may give you a nugget that causes you to stop and think. Or you may get through the entire passage before you stop. The point: think about what you read. Soak it in. Ask God again for understanding if necessary.

P – Preserve. Capture your thoughts on paper or in an email. If you're in an accountability group, exchange discoveries.

T – Thank. Thank God for his Word and for the privilege of spending time with and learning more about him.

OK to photocopy for use in local men's ministries

However you choose to engage with the Bible and encourage other men to become grounded in the Bible, it's worth the effort and the growth you'll see will astound you.

CHAPTER 10

LETTING SCRIPTURE SET THE CULTURE

*H*ow men treat one another changes depending on the environment. Jokes that are fine on fishing trips will get men sent straight to HR at work. Speak as freely with acquaintances as you do with friends and you're asking for trouble.

So how should men treat one another within a men's ministry? Good news: the Bible tells you.

Frequently highlight with you men the passages below, telling men they speak to where you're headed as a ministry. It will be safe to speak honestly when men are living out these values. It will be safe to be themselves. And your meetings will quickly become a favorite place to spend time.

And share this truth, too: These aren't suggestions—they're marching orders.

Men are to love one another

The love of brothers in Christ is one that develops calluses as it finds practical ways to express itself. Consider:
- Men are to be *devoted* to one another ((Romans 12:10)
- Men are to *serve* one another (Galatians 5:13)
- Men are to be *patient* with one another (Ephesians 4:2)

Men are to be unified

In a fractured world your opinionated, sometimes stubborn men are to be unified, experiencing peace. Consider:
- Men are to live in *harmony* (Romans 12:16)

- Men are to *accept* one another (Romans 15:70
- Men are to *forgive* one another (Colossians 3:13)
- Men are to *bear* with each other (Colossians 3:13)

Men are to support each other

Your guys aren't observers in one another's lives—they're participants. They're there to give shoulders to lean on, to lift one another up. Consider:

- Men are to *pray* for each other" (James 4:11)
- Men are to *confess sins* to each other (James 5:16)
- Men are to carry each other's burdens (Galatians 6:2)
- Men are to build each other up (I Thessalonians 5:11)

Men are to live humbly with each other

The world says grab for all the status and power you can reach. The Kingdom says something else. Consider:

- Men are to *serve* each other (John 13:14)
- Men are to *honor* one another (Romans 12:10)
- Men are to *submit* to one another (Ephesians 5:21)
- Men are to *consider others better* than themselves (Philippians 2:3)

CHAPTER 11

STRUCTURING A MEETING

I've said it before and want to say it again: The frequency of your meetings will determine the quality of the relationships your men have with one another.

That's why I encourage meeting weekly. If that's not possible, every two weeks. But if it ends up stretching out to once a month, you're essentially starting from ground zero each month. Based on experience, that's my advice related to the frequency of gatherings.

And since I'm dispensing advice, following are suggestions as to what elements to incorporate into your regular weekly meetings.

The Structure of Weekly Meetings

How you structure your meeting has a direct impact on how your men experience it. And how you'll experience it as well.

Many men's ministries meet in the evening. Especially if men have kids, they aren't available on weekends. And daytime meetings are out because few working men have the flexibility to get away for a few hours mid-day.

So evening it is.

Let's consider how your meeting looks and feels for a typical man in your ministry:

Larry sits behind a desk at the bank and as usual he's up to his elbows in stress. Annoying, demanding customers. A boss with a fistful of unrealistic expectations. Larry brainstorms until his brain hurts, endures pointless, boring meetings, and has to work through lunch. But finally: it's time to call it quits for the day!

Wait. It's Tuesday. The night his men's group meets. Instead of heading home, Larry aims his car toward church where he'll spend a few hours with friends. This is one meeting he actually looks *forward* to attending.

Larry walks into a room buzzing with conversation and smell of barbeque. He can't wait to see what God's got in store for him and the other guys this evening. They'll laugh, talk, sing their hearts out, open their Bibles, and get to know God a little better.

Larry looks around the room and smiles. When it comes to getting together with men, it just doesn't get any better than this!

Larry's right, but here's something he doesn't know: this meeting works well because you and other ministry volunteers and leaders have organized it perfectly. Every element of the meeting has a purpose, and each element is necessary.

Let's walk through what happened behind the scenes.

The Welcome

Men feel comfortable coming into the room because you're there to warmly greet them. You've arranged comfortable seating. There's up-beat, instrumental music playing in the background and the room is well lit. The food is almost ready and smells wonderful.

Everything about this first impression says, "You're wanted here, and this is a safe place. Let go of the day's tensions and enjoy yourself."

The Meal

It may not be fancy, but the food is tasty. And for men watching their calories, you have a healthy alternative to the fried chicken and potato spears. There's plenty to eat, which Larry, whose stomach has been growling since that missed lunch, appreciates.

Eating with other men helps cement friendships. Sitting at a table puts men close together, at the same level, and encourages conversation. Men are connecting and inhibitions fading—guys are opening up as they eat together.

The Fellowship

You make sure new guys get introduced around and keep an eye on the energy in the room. Are men talking? Are they responding to the discussion questions your leader raises?

It takes effort to focus on so many men, but these guys need support and, if they find friends here, they'll have friends who encourage their walk with the Lord.

The Worship

Last week it was singing, this week it's guys calling out things they love about Jesus. Next week it might be something else. But every week there's a way you help men focus on God and express their gratitude for his love.

The Teaching

Guys want to know more about God and the lessons your leaders select meet that need. The man up front is prepared, and it shows. And because he clearly cares, so do the guys in the room.

They listen and they learn, soaking in God's Word.

The Small Groups

The men split into groups and together explore how they'll apply what they've heard. You make a mental note of what the guys in your group say, and you'll follow up next week to ask how it went.

Men challenge each other, support each other, and pray for each other. They're becoming more than friends—they're becoming brothers in Christ.

When Larry heads home after this meeting he's not tired—he's refreshed. And he's smiling. It's been a good night and he's better prepared to deal with his colleagues, more dedicated to being engaged with his family. He feels something powerful flowing in and through him and knows it's more than the satisfaction of a fun evening.

It's the love of Christ.

Your typical meeting may not look quite like what Larry experienced. That's fine. But your meetings will be more effective if they include the elements described here, elements that promote belonging, acceptance, and a deepening faith.

How do you provide a welcoming experience? How do you ensure that fellowship happens, that worship is vibrant and sincere? What do men say about the lessons presented—are they relevant and fresh? And are men growing closer in their small groups? Do you see them affirming and supporting one another? Do you hear stories about them connecting outside of your group time?

Answer those questions and you'll know what steps to take next.

CHAPTER 12

ENGAGING EVENTS

*J*f you're looking to host events that will build a buzz in your community and that your men will be excited to host, you've come to the right place.

Here are a few you might want to add to your ministry's calendar.

Annual Events

Consider holding an annual men's event.

It can be as simple or complex as you'd like. It might be a few hours on a Saturday night at your church, led by your pastors and worship team. Or it might be a weekend event at a campground, complete with fishing, firepits, and guest speakers.

Whatever you choose to do, first ask God if there's a theme or particular Scripture he'd like you to focus on during your event. Or maybe there's a particular book you can lead men through on the weekend.

Our ministry hosted an annual Advance (remember what I said about the word "retreat?") where we led men new to the group through the book, *Wild at Heart* by John Eldredge.

We kicked things off on Friday night at a local church campground. They provided basic, but comfortable, lodging and three meals a day for our men. They also gave us a meeting space and access to a fire pit and a small chapel. A worship team come in to lead us in the evenings.

The schedule included time for individual prayer and reflection after speakers (our leadership team) discussed especially challenging chapters in the book.

Some years, we added "free time" where men could jump into paintball, climb a rock wall, or take a nap. Activities depended on the location.

Yes, there's a fair amount of planning involved. If your ministry is just getting started you might want to wait until you have a bit more manpower before you try to pull off an annual event.

Or just give it a go and see what happens!

Quarterly Meetings

Another way to keep meetings interesting is to plan a quarterly event that's different than your usual meetings.

Our *Wildmen* group met on Tuesday evenings. Typically, there are four months that have five Tuesdays instead of just four. On those extra Tuesdays we did something special for the men. To build excitement we came up with an intriguing, clever name for those nights: Fifth Tuesdays. (Hey, we were tired. And everyone could remember when to show up.)

Maybe the name wasn't special, but the evenings were. Sometimes we set up outside and we had guys bring grills to cook hamburgers or hot dogs. Occasionally, we invited a worship team to lead us in praise and worship.

Once we fed hundreds of men a steak dinner and had Tony Dungy (he was coaching our hometown champions, the Tampa Bay Buccaneers) as a guest speaker. Not only did the men have a fun and memorable time, but the buzz that event created helped expand our reach to the men in our community.

What Events Can Your Ministry Dream?

Get some guys together and, after you pray about it, see what engaging events you can dream up. Don't worry about resources—if the ideas are from God he'll provide what you need to pull off the events.

Following is a list of events I've seen myself or heard men describe. Maybe they'll spark some ideas for your dream team.

Fall Festival

It's like what you do for kids, but man-size it. Live music, plenty of grills, lots of meat, lots of fun. One year, we rented a gladiator bounce house where men could challenge each other to a (safe) duel. We also held an annual home-made pumpkin catapult contest where teams competed for distance, accuracy, and general pumpkin-splatage.

Father's Day Sunday

Check with church leadership to see if the men's ministry can "take over" on Father's Day Sunday. We decorated the stage, selected and performed worship music, and several men tag-teamed the message. We advertised it in the community, and it was a huge draw.

Father-Child/Children Events

Fishing, camping, hiking, paddleboarding—any kind of outdoor adventure can work for some kids. Others might prefer more refined activities like movies, museums, or tea-times (no, not *tee*-times). And you don't necessarily have to deliver some sort of message; kids sharing special times with loving, attentive fathers is message enough.

Football/Baseball/Curling Watch Parties

Root for the home team together while sharing snacks and old sports stories. Extra points to men who can still fit into their old varsity jackets! (And about the curling: someone's got to watch it, right?)

Events are opportunities to re-engage men who've drifted to the outskirts of your group. Recruit them to help plan and pull off the event and they're right back in touch with other men.

And events are newsworthy, too. Announce them in your church and community. See if the local paper or television station wants to risk showing up to cover your pumpkin-catapult competition—their reports will help you connect with your community!

CHAPTER 13

APPROACHING OUTREACH

I'm an old marketing guy, so this facet of men's ministry is near and dear to my heart. It's also right up my alley professionally.

I'll share some basic marketing principles with you. Apply them to your ministry situation and you'll have an effective message to share with the men in your church and community.

Know how to answer the WIIFM question

Be ready when an already busy man looks at you and asks some version of this question: "What's In It For Me?"

It's a reasonable question. You're asking for the man's time and attention; what can he expect to get in return? Why should he become a part of your ministry rather than join the Elks Club?

What he's really asking is what benefits come when men are part of your ministry. In what way are their lives better, their marriages more fulfilling, their hair thicker? Why should a man care what you're doing in the church basement on Tuesday nights?

I can't answer that question for you and I wouldn't if I could. The process of distilling a simple 20-second response will clarify in your mind what your ministry offers and what it's doing in the lives of men. Getting to that quick benefit statement may be challenging, but it's essential for your outreach.

So jot down your response, keep working at it until it's a thing of beauty, and then memorize it.

Because that WIIFM question is coming. I promise.

Make a specific ask

Too many men's ministries confuse making men aware of their ministry with actually asking men to attend a meeting. It's the difference between Mattress Monster announcing they've got mattresses and them asking you to buy one.

Don't just issue blanket invitations; *ask men to show up*. You can't influence men who never actually engage with your ministry.

Add urgency to your ask

There's a reason some television commercials practically scream, "Call now!"

It's because if someone decides to call later that's a call that probably won't happen. People often put things off or forget to circle back.

Special events are perfect for adding urgency to an invite. If guys miss the Chili Cookoff or Pumpkin Catapult Launch those events won't roll around for another year; men have to act now if they want to experience the splendor of Marco's Death by Ghost Pepper Chili or crush a trash can with a ten-pound pumpkin.

On a personal level, don't ask men to consider attending a meeting next month. Offer to pick them up and drive them to *this* week's meeting. That's what my lawyer friend, Mark, did and it's the only reason I showed up at a men's ministry meeting that changed my life.

Advertise (maybe)

Have you priced a billboard or radio commercial lately? Yikes! A full-scale, professional advertising campaign is probably beyond your budget.

Besides, you can reach out other ways that are far cheaper and more effective.

The primary way—and nothing comes close to the impact of this advertising channel—is leveraging personal relationships.

That is, men inviting men. If your guys are talking up your ministry with their buddies at the gym, the office, and in the neighborhood, you'll need to order more food for your next meeting. New guys will come—and they'll come already knowing someone.

So encourage your men to invite others. No amount of TV spots can equal the power of personal invitations.

But if you do choose to advertise, do so strategically to get in front of your two possible target audiences:

1. Men in your church
2. Men in the area who aren't in your church.

Here's how to get to both groups:

Advertising to men within your church

There's probably a process for getting your ministry in front of the whole congregation. Take advantage of whatever you can and don't be afraid to add some flair. For instance, if you're advertising an upcoming men's cookout, make the announcement while wearing an apron and eating a hot dog.

Men will notice!

Here are some advertising options to consider:

- If your church has a monthly calendar, be on it. Every month.
- Use snail mail, sending an invite to every man on the church roll—including those men you haven't seen in a while. Include your phone number and offer to answer questions.
- Sunday bulletins can always use an insert. Make yours fun and colorful.
- If there's a rotating set of announcements up on screen before services, have an announcement about your next special event.
- Spoken announcements can have a huge impact. Ask

your pastor if there's a logical place in the context of an
upcoming sermon where a testimony about how being
in fellowship, or increasing Bible reading, would be
helpful. Offer a man to give a two-minute testimony.

- Set up a "man cave" in the corner of the church lobby
  (a couple recliners should do it) where you're giving
  information to men about your ministry.
- Emails can be effective if you can get them opened.
  Don't be overly clever with your subject line; say
  something like "Check out First Christian Church's
  Guys Only Meeting."
- Post photos and information on the church website and
  Facebook page.
- Ask guys to give their testimonies. As a ministry
  volunteer everyone expects you to be a booster. When
  some guy who attends says the same things they have a
  greater impact.

Advertising to men outside your church

Assuming you're not sitting on a war chest of ad dollars, do this:

- If you have men who are part of community service
  groups, ask that they mention your ministry there.
- Write a letter to the editor of your local paper about
  your group, sharing why it's making a difference and
  how more men are invited. One of the most viewed
  sections of your paper is the editorial page.
- Get listed in the "Community Events" section of free
  newspapers that are often in racks just inside the doors
  of restaurants and grocery stores.
- See if local Christian schools will distribute a take-home
  flyer aimed at dads and grandfathers.
- Take posters to gyms, pubs, and other places men tend
  to congregate. If there's a bulletin board for community
  events, ask that your poster be displayed there.
- Notify other churches that don't have men's ministries.
  Be clear you're not out to pilfer men, just provide a

place where men can grow spiritually.

No matter how you advertise, keep it simple

Keep your message simple in advertisements. Too much information muddles the message. Give the facts and include an invitation—that's all that's needed.

And pray. Always pray

Ask God to bring the men who'll benefit from your ministry. Just be ready to greet them warmly.

CHAPTER 14

BUILDING RELATIONSHIPS

*W*hen Jesus was asked which commandment was greatest, his answer was all about relationships.

He replied, "Love the Lord your God with all your heart and with all your soul and with all your mind and with all your strength.' The second is this: 'Love your neighbor as yourself.' There is no commandment greater than these." (Mark 12: 30-31)

Relationships were at the core of Jesus' message. It's what mattered most then, and what matters most now.

Notice Jesus mentioned two types of relationships.

First, a relationship with the Lord, one in which your men give all they have: heart, soul, mind, and strength. It's this first-priority relationship with God that transforms your men's relationships with people.

When men love God it shows in how they treat others. It increases their capacity to love, serve, and forgive. They experience peace and have the grace to deal with difficult individuals. They're given the wisdom to make tough decisions. They have just the right words when right words aren't easy to find.

The quality of their relationships becomes a testimony to the power of Jesus. John quotes Jesus saying this to his first disciples: "By this everyone will know that you are my disciples, if you love one another." (John 13:35)

So when your men treat one another like the brothers they are, that's a reflection of what Jesus is doing in their hearts. When they reach out across cultural and racial lines, when they put aside politics and focus on faith, that's a sign Jesus is doing something in them.

When their highest-priority relationship is growing, your men are able to love their neighbors like they love themselves.

So be diligent about keeping first things first in your ministry. Double down on helping men build a relationship with Jesus and the rest of their relationships will improve as well.

Following are things you'll see when men focus first on Jesus and then choose to build friendships with one another. Be on the lookout for:

Humility

We men can be proud at times—more interested in ourselves than others. But in Philippians, chapter 2, Paul calls us to regard others as more important than ourselves. We're to look out for the interests of others.

In your ministry that might look like men spending the entire small group time focused on one man who's hurting. It might be take-charge business owners quietly following the lead of a man who's gifted but lacks worldly status.

Relationships thrive when men are humble with one another.

Encouragement

In Ephesians and Colossians, Paul urges us to use only words that are edifying and bring grace to those who listen. Which means in your ministry put-downs, snarky comments, and "just kidding" barbs shouldn't find a home.

In your meetings, watch your language—keep it positive and helpful. Even more, provide encouragement as you help men feel valued. Look them in the eye. Smile. Have an honest interest in their story.

Relationships thrive when men encourage one another.

Persistence

Relationships take effort—and time. As you serve the men in your ministry don't assume they'll quickly befriend you or one another. Let trust build over time. Put a reminder in your calendar to connect with men every so often even if they don't return the favor. Keep the welcome mat to friendship dusted off and visible; there will come a time you make a connection.

Relationships thrive when men are open to friendship.

Remembering

Nothing says, "You matter" more than asking a man how something he mentioned weeks before is working out. It signals you listened, and you care.

Connect with men at special moments in their lives—on a birthday, anniversary, or when you hear their kids won a scholarship or spelling bee.

And while you're at it, learn the names of men's wives and children.

Relationships thrive when men pay attention to one another and remember.

Confidentiality

Relationships seldom survive betrayal, and a man who shares something in small group will almost certainly feel betrayed if it leaks. Trust is slow to build but can be shredded in one careless moment.

Keep confidences not so secrets can be hidden, but so it's safe to share them.

Relationships thrive when men trust they can share openly.

Brokenness

Every one of your men is broken in some way but not every man is willing to admit it or humbly ask for help. Some men (maybe most) would rather give than receive help.

As a volunteer, model vulnerability. Admit failures and let guys comfort you, confess sin and ask men to pray for you. Don't worry about falling off a pedestal; it's not likely anyone has you on one anyway.

In a healthy men's ministry there's some "ugly" comes with the beauty. Expect it and join men in seeking answers from God when it arrives.

Relationships thrive when men both minister to others and receive ministry from others.

Fun

If all you ever talk about is hard stuff, how long do you expect men to stick around?

Do fun things together. Discover mutual interests and pursue them side by side. Workouts? Music? Motors? Sports? It's great to have someone around who's as passionate about your interests as you are.

Relationships thrive when men have fun together.

CHAPTER 15

HAVING EFFECTIVE SMALL GROUPS

*E*verything in your ministry comes down to small group time. That's where men connect most closely with each other. Where they engage and challenge one another. Where they discover they're not the only ones dealing with tough stuff and ongoing issues.

It's where men pray for one another and support each other.

Get your ministry's small groups right and your men will grow as they:

- Find and form new friendships
- Discover their spiritual gifts
- Develop both leadership and a willingness to serve
- Share needs, frustration, and concerns
- Explore and apply God's Word and
- Pray, praise, and worship God with likeminded men

Keep in mind not all men are ready for the relational intensity of a small group in which men share honestly and openly. It takes time for mutual trust to build. Small group leaders—and that may or may not be your volunteer role—have to ease men toward the deep end of the transparency pool.

Even if you're not the leader, you can help by both modeling honest sharing and being an attentive listener. Men open up more quickly when they believe someone wants to hear what they have to say.

Here are a few tips I've learned from years in men's ministry small groups:

Allow ample time

Small group sharing is often the last thing on the meeting agenda, so every minute a speaker goes long and every extra song tossed in by the worship team eats away at the time small groups have together.

Don't let small group time be an afterthought. Aim for a minimum of thirty minutes for small group time. That's about long enough for men to check in, discuss the teaching, and pray for one another.

Let the Holy Spirit lead

It's important to stay on schedule but more important to let the Holy Spirit lead your small group time. Sure, you want to get through a few questions from the evening's study guide, but if a hurting man opens up and gets personal toss the questions aside.

There's a balance here. As your men speak, ask the Holy Spirit to take the reins. You probably don't want it to happen every week, but if a guy needs to get something off his chest let it happen and allow your guys to minister to one another.

Don't be too quick to quench what may turn out to be a pivotal moment in a man's life.

Pray

One of the best things you can do for the men in your small group is to pray for them regularly.

Mention each man by name. Keep a journal of prayer requests, praises, and concerns. You'll find that, as you pray for your men, God will strengthen your relationships.

A reminder: Confidentiality includes not telling others outside the group your men's' prayer requests.

Limit Group Size

With just 30 to 45-minutes for small group time, you've got

to keep groups small. With ten men in a group if each guy takes two minutes just to check in, you're at 20-minutes before diving into anything meaty. I've found that once a group gets to eight men, it's time to split into two small groups and grow from there.

Talk with leadership about how men new to the ministry will join small groups. Once a group is established, adding new members can sometimes be disruptive, resetting the trust clock to zero. But new guys have to go somewhere, right?

Another wrinkle: our ministry encouraged men to stay in the same group from week to week so friendships could deepen. I saw other ministries form completely new groups each week, the advantage being that men met new guys each week.

Ask your leadership to reach decisions about which ways to go with integrating new men and how often—if ever—to switch around group members.

Provide Training

Invest in small group leaders with occasional training. In *Wildmen* we held quarterly meetings for small group leaders.

Two reasons:

First and foremost, it's a good excuse to get small group leaders together to discuss what's working and not working in their groups.

Second, we found taking leadership tests and personality evaluations helped small group leaders understand their strengths, weaknesses, and why they might find connecting with specific group members challenging.

Report to Leadership

One disadvantage of breaking into groups is that ministry leaders lose visibility into what's happening. Overcome this by establishing a reporting structure so small groups let leaders know what's up in small groups.

It can be as easy as an email from small group leaders to ministry leaders. It can be a weekly check in or maybe your leaders just want updates if something especially good or bad has happened.

Have a way to let other small groups know if one of your guys needs help moving or could use backup while dealing with another significant issue. You can notify ministry leaders and let them spread the word or set up a small group leader email group and spread the word yourself.

And yet again: Confidentiality. Share nothing with other small group letters without permission from the man involved in the issue.

Communicate often—even more often than that

I was a small group leader in a men's ministry that had a half-dozen groups. Each week, I emailed my guys a list of prayer concerns that had been mentioned the previous evening. I also thanked my men for fighting through their days to be at our meeting.

The day before our next meeting, I sent another short email reminding my guys about the meeting and telling them how excited I was for us to be together again.

After a month, guys in my group were still faithfully attending and we'd formed close friendships. In other groups men attended less frequently and were still taking relational baby steps.

When small group leaders connect often with their men, good things happen.

Small group leaders can also take it to the next level by having coffee with each of their guys each month. Or occasionally taking a guy out for breakfast. If leaders and group members share a passion for golf or hiking, those are great activities to do together.

My point: look for opportunities to communicate and do life together.

Always be training co-leaders

If your ministry is going to grow, you need a steady supply of trained small group leaders, so mentor guys now. Pick a guy in each group and get that guy ready to take on his own group.

Give those co-leaders actual responsibilities, by the way—don't just have them observe. And when training happens co-leaders have co-leaders there, too.

Dos and don'ts for small group discussion

Do remind men about confidentiality. A mention each week reminds guys who've been coming and sets an expectation for new men.

Don't do all the talking. If you're a small group leader be a discussion facilitator. Watch for men who talk too much, those who aren't talking at all, and gently shut down guys who monopolize the sharing time. Invite quiet men into the conversation by asking if there's anything they'd like to add.

Do be an active listener. Listen with your eyes and heart as well as your ears. And always be listening for the Holy Spirit—invite him into every conversation.

Don't fear silence. Sometimes those silent moments are when the Holy Spirit is moving, or guys are thinking. Twenty seconds of silence may seem like an eternity, but it's often followed by great inspiration.

Do use open ended questions. Avoid yes/no or true/false questions. Recast questions so they encourage dialog. Also, ask follow-up questions. For example, follow up an answer with, "I wonder why you say that" or "How would you explain your answer to a non-Christian friend?"

Do be aware of the doctrine-cop. That's the guy who just can't wait to make a theological point or set guys straight on a doctrinal issue. Shut him down with love, but also with firmness.

Do watch out for the insensitive guy. If someone is

correcting, making fun of, or cutting off men, it can easily offend and disrupt your group. Remind your group everyone's thoughts and doubts are welcome and you're all in this together. Later, outside of group, talk to offenders about their behavior. Do your best to affirm them as well.

CHAPTER 16

FOSTERING CONFIDENTIALITY
AND ACCOUNTABILITY

*I*f your idea of men's ministry is an occasional pancake breakfast where conversations are mostly "pass the syrup," don't worry about confidentiality—nothing will be said that's deep or personal.

And accountability won't be on the menu.

But if you want to see men develop deep friendships that stand the test of time, relationships where men share their "this is keeping me up at night" stuff, you've got to instill both accountability and confidentiality into your ministry.

Here's how to encourage confidentiality:

Set the expectation early and often

We announce it at every men's ministry meeting: what's said at the meeting is confidential. Nothing said is to be talked about with wives, children, with others in the church, with others *period*.

One person with loose lips can sabotage months, even years, of relationship building. It's critical to remind your men how important this is every time you meet.

Put it in writing

The covenant you'll find at the end of this chapter spells out what "confidentiality" means in practical terms. Have men sign this covenant. Even better, bring a long a stamp pad and have them also affix a thumbprint over their signature.

Realize there may be leaks

Businesses use confidentiality agreements so they can sue employees who carry business secrets with them when they leave. Your ministry won't be taking anyone to court. Be clear the purpose of an agreement is to clarify understanding, not to threaten legal action.

And tell men that if, in a careless moment they share something they shouldn't, to let the group know, so they can be forgiven.

Here are ways to encourage accountability among your men:

Give men time to become friends

Accountability implies men are sharing significant stuff, telling one another their intentions. That only happens after men trust one another and trust starts with friendship. So give guys time to hang out, share meals, and listen to and pray for one another. That's what gets the friendship ball rolling.

Encourage honesty

When you create a safe place, honesty follows. And often the best way to foster honesty is for small group leaders and other volunteers—like you—to model it. As you share your weaknesses, struggles, and questions, others will be encouraged to do the same.

Value your men

Look for opportunities to build up your men and encourage others to do the same. Men who consider each other valuable and important will work hard to respect their commitments to one another.

Expect accountability

Introduce accountability questions into small group discussions. These are questions that move past generalities to become specific and personal—but not nosy.

It's a balancing act but this will help you know if you're on solid ground: Are the questions you ask for the benefit of your men or to satisfy your curiosity? The first are fine, the second not so much.

Be accountable to the right things

Make sure the men are being held accountable to God's standards, not the opinions of another man in the group. One way to stay calibrated in this regard is to insert this question into discussions: "What does God's word say about this topic?"

Be lavish with grace

A man might tell you he's going to do it this time—he's really going to give up porn/gambling/sarcasm/something else. And he *means* it. He's *serious*.

Just like he said he was giving it up.

When men fail to keep their promises to themselves or you, be as gracious with them as God is with you. Stand them up, brush them off, and help them try again, learning what there is to learn from the latest failure.

And this time leaning even more on the power of Christ.

Move slowly

A few questions to encourage accountability, a habit of following up to see if promises are kept, actively praying for men to be transformed. They're all good moves but none of them are necessarily quick moves.

So be patient. Accountability will come.

If you want to begin introducing accountability questions here are a few to consider:

Questions about a man's relationship with God

- How is your relationship with God changing—or isn't it?
- How have you seen God at work in your life this past week?
- In what ways are your finances reflecting your commitment to God?
- What areas of your life might be hindering your relationship with God?
- When you prayed this past week, what did you pray about and why?

Questions about activities

- How are you showing love to your family members?
- In what ways have your words or actions hurt someone this week?
- What's something that would help you spiritually if you stopped doing it?
- What's something that would help you grow spiritually if you did it?
- How might you step out in faith in this coming week?

Questions about men's interior lives

- In what ways have you faced temptation lately? What happened?
- How comfortable would you be having your browser history known? Why?
- How did you experience disappointment or loneliness this week?
- What's keeping you up at night? What are worries and stresses in your life?
- Where in life are you harboring bitterness or anger?
- What's one thing you believe God is calling you to do that you've not done?

And two questions to ask after men have answered

accountability questions in a small group setting:
- Are you hiding anything for which you need to be accountable?
- Have you lied about any of the questions you've answered today?

Notice how all but the last two questions—which need to be pointed and direct—are open-ended. They invite men to share. They don't attempt to catch men out but rather invite them in.

In, to experience honest communication. In, to confession and forgiveness for shortcomings. In, to the joy of being vulnerable and accountable with men who love them.

Sample Covenant

As a member of First Christian's men's ministry, I will:
- Show respect by being on time to meetings and events.
- Keep things said in group discussions confidential.
- Make meetings a priority and attend as faithfully as possible.
- Participate in group discussions, while being careful not to dominate.
- Respect others at all times, especially when there's disagreement or conflict.
- Help others and be available outside of group meetings whenever possible.

OK to photocopy for use in local men's ministries

CHAPTER 17

SERVING TOGETHER

*S*erving together creates bonds among men. They'll be sharing stories about their service projects for years to come. Plus, the spiritual rewards received from serving the "least of these" in your community are well documented in scripture.

Here are 35 ideas to consider when planning to serve your community:

Oil Changes for Single Moms

If you've got some mechanically inclined men, offer free oil changes for cash-strapped single moms. See if a local auto repair shop will partner with you for this much-appreciated gift.

Community Service Day

Several churches in my area band together each spring to perform general cleanup, yard work, and simple home repairs for those most in need of the service. This idea started out small and now provides services to hundreds of needy families. A perfect place for your men's group to launch.

Adopt A School

A church in a fairly rough area of Tampa has worked with a nearby school for years. As school officials came to trust men in the church, the breadth of service expanded. Now it includes care of the school grounds, simple repairs of school property, and providing backpacks of supplies to low-income students.

Community Service

This one isn't simple, but your men could start out small and grow it from there.

A church I'd just started attending kept talking about a huge outreach weekend that was scheduled soon. I wasn't completely sure what to expect but on the appointed morning I showed up at a Walmart in a poorer part of town.

I found a large rectangle of tents—the kind you might see at an art show or farmer's market. Each tent provided those in this community with much-needed services, such as:

- A photographer who shot free family portraits
- Hairdressers who provided complimentary haircuts for kids and adults
- Mental Health Counselors who made their services available at no cost
- A team skilled at making repairing bicycles
- A mini thrift store where people could select free clothing and toiletries
- Professional resume writers and employment coaches who helped people prepare for interviews
- Prayer warriors who listened to and prayed with anyone who wanted it

Word spread quickly and by early afternoon, the place was swarming with area residents, each being ministered to in the way that person needed most.

It was an amazing site to see.

In the evening, leaders of the event soon took to the stage and welcomed everyone—including kids who knew what was about to happen.

Volunteers had gathered donations of new bicycles, toys, stuffed animals, and games. There were gifts for adults, too, like new televisions and coffee makers.

A worship band gave an incredible concert and simple gospel presentation. When the crowd was asked who wanted to know Jesus, nearly every hand went up. They *all* wanted to know Jesus.

Volunteers prayed with each person and invited them back to the same location the next morning where they could get on a bus to take them to a place they could be baptized.

Up until that day, I'd never seen—or even heard of—such a tangible demonstration of the love and grace of Jesus.

Attempting a service project like this might be beyond the reach of your men's ministry right now, but what might a scaled down version look like?

Block Party

Invite families from the streets around your church building to come by on a Saturday afternoon for games, bounce castles, hot dogs fresh off the grill, and the chance to meet their neighbors.

Host a One-Day Vacation Bible School in a neighborhood park

Get your guys on board to do a stripped-down version of the VBS you hold at church in one day. Be sure all guys get a background check before they work with kids.

Host meals for international students

Are you near a college? Get the word out that you'll be serving up typical local meals and giving foreign students the chance to practice their conversational English.

Become fast food friends

Drive-through sack lunches aren't always the healthiest, but for someone isolated at home a Bucky Burger from Bennie's Burger Shack might be just the ticket. Contact home-bound church members to find out what they'd like for lunch and pick up and deliver the order along with whatever the guy making the burger run wants to eat. The catch: Your guy and the home-bound church member will eat together.

Cooking classes

Have access to a church kitchen that's seldom used? Do what Jennifer did—offer a gluten-free cooking class.

Jennifer has celiac disease, a condition that means she can't tolerate gluten. She knew other celiacs struggled to bake bread, make pasta, and otherwise cope with their strict diet so she posted on a neighborhood Facebook page she'd be giving a cooking demonstration in the church kitchen. She showed up that Saturday to find a line at the door.

Do you have men who could lead a workshop? Cooking… wood carving…laptop virus removal…see what your men can do and then get a few guys together to lead and support the workshop.

Exercise Classes

Instead of offering a typical exercise class, how about designing one especially for seniors? If you don't have a qualified instructor in your group, partner with a local health club or agency to set up in your church building once a week to teach seniors how to stretch and strengthen their bodies. Your men can be cheerleaders!

Community Garden

If you've got an outside water tap and the ability to rototill turf, you've got what you need to host a community garden that helps feed your neighborhood. Ask men to pair up and take turns caring for the garden.

Job Fair/Career Counseling/Resume Assistance

From editing resumes to providing practice interviews, this is a service that's desperately needed by some people who are terrified of entering or re-entering the job market. What men are in your ministry who could help?

Set Up a Clothes Closet or Food Pantry

This takes work—and there may be city ordinances governing what you can and can't do, but your men can look into this. If establishing a closet or pantry is too much, how about owning a regular slot on the schedule of existing closets or pantries?

Here's a quick list of more service possibilities for your men's ministry:

- Organize Operation Christmas Child or Angel Tree for your congregation
- Pull together a community yard sale
- Host a seasonal festival for kids
- Organize a health fair
- Hold a First Responders breakfast
- Organize a blood drive for the church or community
- Do light janitorial duty following services
- Set up rooms for weddings, dinners, special events
- Decorate the church building for holidays
- Organize and staff a church "Trunk or Treat" for Halloween
- Create or curate art exhibits in the lobby of your church building
- Meet to fold church bulletins, staple sermon notes pages, or other easy-to-chat-while-doing-it tasks
- Take packaged goodies to police stations and fire departments for their break rooms
- Create birthday party boxes for use at homeless shelters
- Do a diaper drive for a local pregnancy center
- Help a refugee family navigate registering kids for school and

filling out paperwork
- Cheer like crazy at a Special Olympics event
- Host a high tea for young children to attend with their parents—extra points for guys who wear aprons
- Organize a gingerbread house building event
- Clear the parking lot and ask a local classic car club to do a show
- Host a trivia night for church families
- Create a newsletter for senior adults in your church

Notice that each of these service projects can be done by groups of men or, at minimum, a pair of men.

That's key—have men serve *together*. It's a huge relationship enhancer!

CHAPTER 18

STRENGTHENING MARRIAGES

*Y*ou've probably heard that divorce rates among Christians are just as high as among non-Christians.

It's a bit more nuanced than that.

One study took a close look at those early statistics and found that "'active conservative protestants who attend church regularly are actually 35% less likely to divorce than those who have no religious preferences.'"[6]

So, at least in some Christian circles, marriages seem to be doing well, or at least not as badly as elsewhere in our society.

Bottom line: In your men's ministry you'll encounter men whose marriages are in trouble…or failing. That will be a crisis you need to cope with.

Other men will be in marriages that are unfulfilling or that they're essentially ignoring. Those men aren't facing divorce—yet. There's still time for your men's ministry to support them as they fix what's broken in their marriages.

A caution: Your ministry is not a counseling practice. You may find you're quickly out of your depth when it comes to helping men mend their marriages. So have a few counselors to whom you can refer men, counselors who can provide professional services.

---

6   As quoted by Stetzer, Ed. "The Exchange." Christianity Today. "Marriage, Divorce, and the Church: What do the stats say, and can marriage be happy?"

Your ministry can still help build stronger marriages, though, and here's how:

Talk and teach about marriage

It's a little tricky doing extensive teaching about marriage in your men's group if there are unmarried men, but you won't be faulted for dealing with the topic of marriage from time to time.

If you engage in a marriage-related study with your men, small group discussions will be extremely helpful—especially if men have had time to develop trust. That trust will allow men to ask one another questions, to speak honestly to one another, and to gently help men see where they've wandered off track as husbands.

Especially when dealing with topics like marriage, confidentiality is critical. Remind your men of this often.

Help husbands fill the proper tank

One of the most effective tools I've seen help husbands and wives understand each other is Gary Chapman's book, *The Love Languages of God.*

My good friend, Dr. TJ Ammons, is a pastor, men's ministry leader, and marriage counselor. "My love language is acts of service and my wife's is quality time," he says. "So, I'm outside cutting the grass, inside washing dishes, doing all these things trying to earn her love. And then she says she wishes I'd just come inside and sit with her."

TJ says that's like trying to fill a tank that's not there. When TJ works with married couples he emphasizes each person in the marriage must understand what the other's needs are.

Men won't automatically know—but you can encourage them to find out and a capable counselor or week reading about love languages can do the trick. It's stunning how quickly a marriage can improve when men begin loving their wives in the way their wives most feel loved.

Don't make busy men too busy

Some men's ministries expect men to meet weekly as a group, to meet with a small group weekly, and attend quarterly special events.

At some point, it's too much.

Meet frequently, but not so often wives begin feeling squeezed out by your schedule. Keep a finger on the pulse of your men's marriages. Be sure your meetings are helping.

Provide childcare for a couples' date night

Your guys as babysitter? Sure—why not?

Recruit some brave men to take over the church nursery and a few rooms where they can lead games, read story books, and otherwise entertain kids. Then let married couples know there's free babysitting for up to three hours on a particular evening.

Ask the children's ministry workers in your church to advise you about how many kids you can responsibly care for and what you need to do to clean up the rooms you use. Forgetting to empty the diaper pail will not be easily or quickly forgiven.

Host a Married Couples Event

Our ministry hosted an amazing marriage event one year. It started on Friday night on Valentine's weekend and ended Saturday afternoon. Gary Smalley was our special guest speaker.

Try hosting a similar event and offer free babysitting, dinner served by the church's youth group (maybe as a fund raiser?), and you can substitute a video message as an alternative to a special guest speaker if you're on a budget.

At one such event the men leapt up during the meal, walked up on stage, and serenaded their wives. Unbeknownst to the ladies, their husbands had been meeting weekly to practice a medley of cheesy love songs. Mushy? You bet. Appreciated? Here's a hint: that "surprise serenade" was repeated year after year at the Valentine's banquet.

CHAPTER 19

REINFORCING FATHER/CHILD BONDS

*T*he impact a men's ministry can have in the lives of children can be life-altering and long-lasting.

That's true as fathers in your ministry choose to be ever more intentional about being with their own children, and also true if men in your group spend time with children whose fathers are absent.

Any child who has a connection with a loving and attentive father, or who's influenced by an adult male stepping into that father role, is pointed toward the heavenly Father.

Let's talk first about the dads and stepdads in your ministry.

In your role as a volunteer you probably don't know how your guys are doing as dads. Prayer requests will tell you a lot, as will comments that arise in conversation. But don't wait until you hear that men are struggling before helping fathers be fathers. Be pro-active—ask men where their role is challenging. Provide resources before guys start floating past on life-rafts because the Good Ship Fatherhood is sinking.

• **Host a seminar** specifically about Christian fathering, bringing in a counselor to lead. The guys who need to be there will show up.

• **Make fathering resources available.** A brief list is in Chapter 24.

• **Call fathers up front** and, as a group, pray for them and their call to turn the hearts of their children toward God.

• **Consider hosting a dads' discussion group.** Invite dads to share what's working and not working when it comes to raising their children.

And then look around your congregation. Are there children whose fathers are absent for some reason? If so, connect with their moms and ask if they'd like to have one or more of your men occasionally spend time with their kids.

Yes, I know how loaded and potentially creepy that request might sound.

So before you move ahead, ask your children's ministry leader about guidelines for spending time with children. And check with your local Big Brothers/Big Sisters office to get their advice, too.

At minimum be sure no child is ever alone with one of your guys unless that guy has a current clean background check—and maybe not even then. It's probably okay for a child to join several of your men (or a married couple) on public outings.

Outings like:

- Taking in or even making a movie
- Going fishing
- Building something together
- Attending a concert
- Going out for pizza or ice cream
- Bringing kids so together you can do chores for a senior who needs help
- Taking in a baseball game or other sporting event
- Attending the child's school play, baseball game, or other event
- Having a child over for a home-cooked meal and glimpse at how a Jesus follower treats his wife and kids

Whatever the activity, use it to get to know the child. Ask open-ended questions. Help the child feel seen, heard, and valued. And pray with and for the child.

And then follow up. Forging or deepening a relationship may take two, three, or more efforts. Eventually kids will understand your men really care—and that moment is a game changer.

A way to walk alongside your group's dads who have older sons is to help those sons transition to manhood with a Coming-of-Age ritual.

Celebrate Coming of Age

Some cultures have clearly defined traditions that transition males from "child" to "man" status.

In the Vanuatu culture boys hurl themselves from a 30-meter towers with vines tied around their ankles. Aborigine boys trek across Australian wilderness alone for as long as six months to be recognized as men.

In other cultures it's circumcision or a ceremony like a Jewish Bar Mitzvah.

In our culture it's—what? Getting a driver's license? Going on a date? Turning 18 or 21? How do boys know when they become men?

In his book, *Raising a Modern Day Knight*, Robert Lewis suggests several ceremonies your men could adapt to welcome young men into the company of men. And part of that process can be having teenage boys spend time with men in your group so those boys can understand what it means to be a man in God's eyes.

Consider it a homework assignment to answer this question: How can your men's ministry help shape the values and set the standards in the lives of young men?

Let me know where your answer to that question leads you.

CHAPTER 20

SHARING FAITH IN A MAN-FRIENDLY WAY

There are a hundred approaches to sharing the Gospel. Some involve asking leading questions that pry open opportunities to preach. Others encourage ongoing service that eventually prompts a question about why you're so helpful. Bingo! Tell that person about Jesus.

I considered laying out a few of those and suggesting your men practice them. Which will, if they're like many Christian men, absolutely terrify your guys.

Many men aren't convinced they know enough Scripture to share their faith. Or live a pure enough life to share their faith. Or, truth be told, if they want to *risk* sharing their faith—they're afraid of alienating friends and family.

So don't ask men to share their faith.

Instead, ask them to share their *story*.

And their story goes like this: *Before I knew Jesus (or was serious about him instead of religion), I was like _____. Then I met Jesus. And now I'm _____. Not perfect, but _____.*

That testimony of life change is powerful because the guy sharing it is standing right there saying what happened. Nobody can argue with that man's story. They can argue against his position, question his facts, or even attack his beliefs.

But his story? That's bullet-proof, and it's a testimony of the transforming power of the living God in the life of a man.

If you want to see how that approach to sharing the Gospel looks in Scripture, read chapter 9 in the book of John.

All the questions the man will hear after he shares his story can be answered with a simple, "I'm not sure how to answer some of your questions, but I'm happy to introduce you to some people who might be able to speak into them. How about coming to our next men's ministry meeting?" Or the invite can be to church.

Your guys will do that.

Even the ones who are terrified of theological discussions.

At some meeting in the near future have men figure out what they'd say if they were to tell their story using that simple "I was, I met Jesus, I am" formula. Once they have it down, God will open opportunities to share their faith.

CHAPTER 21

WELCOMING NEW MEN

*Y*ou asked and now they've come. They're standing just inside the doorway looking around, wondering what's next.

So how do you turn these visitors into regulars?

Let me state right up front that your ministry isn't going to be for everyone. A guy may show up and decide he doesn't like it. That's okay.

Lots of different sorts will check you out. You may see motorcycle-riders and sports enthusiasts. Paddleboarders and hikers. Technology nerds and gamers whose favorite activity is coming back inside.

Not everyone will feel at home—but you can stack the odds in your favor if you're actually welcoming.

If a guy pulls into the church parking lot and can't figure out what door to go in, that's not welcoming. If he walks in and finds cliques of guys huddled together, nobody waving him over or walking up to greet him, that's not welcoming. If all guys talk about is an event this newbie didn't attend, or crack inside jokes he can't possibly understand, that's not welcoming.

You've got to do better. And here's how...

Make a good first impression

It starts with making sure your meeting can be easily found through signage and perhaps a guy outside to wave men in. Have a greeter or two say "Hi" and then go the extra step of introducing a new guy around.

Make the room guy-friendly

If there are lace doilies on little tables, switch rooms. Now.

If possible decorate your place to look (but not smell) a bit like a man cave. We had a mounted moose head we named Pierre that we'd drag out of a closet each week to hang on the wall.

Your environment can be a deal breaker for some visitors. You don't need to cater to the more masculine guys by hauling Harleys up on stage but do make the room comfortable for guys.

As in deep-six those doilies.

Value visitors

Get their contact information and send a "thanks for coming" text or email the next day.

At your meeting, listen. Smile. Ask questions. Explain things. Affirm comments. Ask for feedback. All these make visitors feel valued and make it more likely they'll return.

And if visitor doesn't return for the next meeting, contact him and let him know he's welcome back.

Plug new guys in

Have at least a few small groups that know they may be hosting newbies. Don't let a new guy miss out on the experience of men having refreshingly honest and caring conversations. He may not join in the first meeting, but you can be sure he's taking it all in, and may want more of it.

Make intentional connections

If you're talking to a new guy about his hobbies and discover he's an avid skeet shooter, introduce him to Brian, that skeet-shooting guy who's also in your group. They may never go out and blast a few clay pigeons, but your visitor will have someone to talk to who understands him a bit.

You can't make connections without engaging visitors and asking questions. And that's not just your job. It's the responsibility of every volunteer. Actually, every man in the ministry needs to notice visitors and step into conversations with them.

Failure to do so turns that door visitors walked through into a revolving door because they can leave just as fast as they came in.

CHAPTER 22

BLESSING YOUR CHURCH

*A*s a volunteer in your men's ministry, you know how transformed men bless their families and can bless other men. But your ministry can also bless your entire congregation—and here's how that can happen...

Transformed men become leaders

Your ministry can become a training ground for up and rising leaders as men assume responsibility for small groups, for leading worship, for teaching and facilitating. Those are all skills that can be used elsewhere in your church.

Transformed men become servants

In the context of your ministry men will disciple others, mentor counsel, and visit in hospitals and homes. They'll do the work of ministry humbly and well.

And instead of ministries begging from the platform for volunteers, your men will actively seek serving opportunities and step in to meet them.

Transformed men pick up their hammers

If there's a worn-out wooden deck that needs replacing, you've probably got men who can do it. If leaves and branches are cluttering up the church property, your guys can clear the debris. An older couple downsizing and needing muscle on a Saturday morning to move those sofas? No problem.

Men focused on ministry are happy to serve their faith community—especially if there's fresh lemonade involved.

God uses transformed men to make things happen

The church where *Wildmen* was launched benefited from new ministries sprouting up along the way, such as several men who took charge of emergency preparedness. They even became volunteer first responders in their community.

Several men took fatherless boys on an adventure each month, giving those young men role models and access to men who loved Jesus.

A couple of the men trained in law enforcement became a church security team, diligent to protect the flock in an age of live shooter situations.

One of our original ministry members got an opportunity to visit Africa on a mission trip. He returned sensing a calling to raise money to benefit that ministry and now he runs multiple Christian schools in an African country.

Stay mindful your ministry isn't an island unto itself. Seek to serve not just one another, but also your larger church. You're part of the larger Body of Christ, too.

CHAPTER 23

IN CASE OF EMERGENCY

*T*here's not a safety manual on the planet that could cover every possible emergency scenario that might arise in a men's ministry.

My friend Steve tells about the time that, at an Advance, one of his guys got hooked in the posterior by another man while the two were fly fishing. Steve wasn't about to add "De-Hooking Buns" to the Advance Handbook between "Campfire Care" and "Heimlich Maneuver How-To's."

So we'll keep things general.

As a ministry volunteer be ready to respond should you encounter:

Health Crises

Basic first aid training is a must for volunteers like you. Contact your local Red Cross office to find out what training is available and at minimum become certified in CPR. Carry a basic first aid kit when your guys are on outings, too.

Find out which of your guys has medical training of some sort. It's a good guess firefighters, police officers, and hospital staffers are first responders but other men may have training, too.

And a question for your ministry leaders: Should a signed release be required for men to attend an Advance or take part in service projects?

Abuse

The National Council on Aging reports that about one in 10 Americans aged 60 or older have suffered some type of elder abuse. If you have older men in your ministry watch for abuse symptoms such as bruises, cuts, or broken bones; poor hygiene; malnourishment or weight loss; unexplained loss of money; anxiety, depression, confusion; or withdrawal from family members or friends.[7]

If you suspect elder abuse notify your ministry leader immediately. If you *are* the ministry leader, report your suspicions to the police. You may not be a mandatory reporter, but you are committed to act in the best interest of your men.

Cognitive Health Crises

Many men's ministries attract older men who have time to participate and are hungry for human connection. So you may encounter cognitive health issues.

It takes a professional to diagnose dementia, but early symptoms include significant memory loss, difficulty in completing familiar tasks, and confusion regarding time or place.[8]

If you notice these issues arising in a man's life, don't offer an uninformed diagnosis. But do make a mental note to check with a person in that man's life who might be able to tell you if their senior has a cognitive health issue.

Crises of Faith

Men are often hesitant to admit they no longer have the same confidence in God they once had. Letting unanswered questions pile up has a tendency to erode faith—so don't let it happen.

---

7   Signs of Elder Abuse - Know Warning Signs of Elderly Abuse (nursinghomeabusecenter.com)

8   Get the Facts on Healthy Aging (ncoa.org)

If you suspect a man is on shaky ground, ask about it. Don't let shame or fear keep doubts locked away where they can eat at a man. Simply saying, "I noticed you didn't seem sure about life after death when it came up in our lesson. Are you wondering if that's really in your future?" will invite a conversation.

Don't judge or condemn but do remind men of the truth and gently point them to scriptures that deal with the issue at hand. And don't expect one conversation to settle an issue; be willing to come back to it again.

If a man is considering walking away from God take it seriously. Find out now who you can bring into the conversation—a ministry leader or pastor, perhaps.

In men's ministry we're here to hold one another up during hard times. Experiencing doubt is one of those times.

Getting ready for an emergency—what does that look like?

Glad you asked.

In addition to suggestions above, here's a cheat sheet for responding to emergencies.

Pray

Ask God how he'd have you respond to the issue in front of you. You probably can't fix it; what role do you have in supporting the person who's hurting?

Pray, and, if it doesn't cross confidentiality lines, ask others to pray as well.

Seek counsel

Who can you call at midnight to help you sort out what to do? As a ministry volunteer, you need that phone number. It may be your small group coordinator, your pastor, or a level-headed friend, but *have that number.*

And don't use it until you need it.

Turn to scripture

Share encouragement from God's Word with hurting people who are ready to hear it, but don't forget to give a hug, too.

Act (and act quickly)

Make your way to the hospital waiting room. Call to let someone know you care. You may not have been asked for help, but that doesn't mean you can't offer it.

Report and/or refer

If you're out of your depth let someone better equipped handle the situation. Your best assistance may be finding qualified help and helping the hurting person make contact. And if in your judgment someone is at risk of harming either themselves or others, getting immediate help supersedes your commitment to confidentiality.

Not every emergency is a crisis—yet

Here are a few small situations that can become major crises if you don't deal with them right away:

• Containing the verbose

There's one in every group: a guy not too shy to share. Once he gets started, he won't quit talking. Deal with this by opening discussions with an expectation such as, "In a sentence or two, how would you answer this…" It may also help to sit next to him so a hand on his shoulder or eye contact signals it's time to let someone else talk. If the behavior continues, talk with him about it—outside the group time.

• Calming the argumentative

Guidelines help here. If your group has a covenant, make sure it mentions respect for others' opinions. Let the argumentative know small group time is not for vigorous debate, or political or doctrinal grandstanding. Gently interrupt, sum up what the guy is saying, and move on by asking others for their thoughts.

• Helping the broken hearted

Small group time should never be about one man but if a guy needs extra grace, is willing to share, and the Holy Spirit is nudging you to let it play out—do so. You're giving men the chance to minister to one of their own. But if a guy expects small time to be a weekly therapy session, outside of the group address the issue and make a referral to a more appropriate place to get help.

And because God's Word is always the right place to find help…

Following are a those passages you'll want handy. They address issues men commonly face:

Accepting Change

And we know that in all things God works for the good of those who love him, who have been called according to his purpose. (Romans 8:28)

Comfort

"Come to me, all you who are weary and burdened, and I will give you rest." (Matthew 11:28)

Contentment

Keep your lives free from the love of money and be content with what you have, because God has said, "Never will I leave you; never will I forsake you." (Hebrews 13:5)

Dealing with Death

Now if we died with Christ, we believe that we will also live with him. For we know that since Christ was raised from the dead, he cannot die again; death no longer has mastery over him. (Romans 6:8-9)

Depression

God is our refuge and strength, an ever-present help in trouble. Therefore we will not fear, though the earth give way and the mountains fall into the heart of the sea.... (Psalm 46:1-2)

Encouragement

Wait for the Lord; be strong and take heart and wait for the Lord. (Psalm 27:14)

Fear

The Lord is my light and my salvation—whom shall I fear? The Lord is the stronghold of my life—of whom shall I be afraid? (Psalm 27:1)

Grief

The Lord is close to the brokenhearted and saves those who are crushed in spirit. (Psalm 34:18)

Hope

Be strong and take heart, all you who hope in the Lord. (Psalm 31:24)

Loneliness

I will not leave you as orphans; I will come to you. (John 14:18)

Money

> *And my God will meet all your needs according to the riches of his glory in Christ Jesus. (Philippians 4:19)*

Peace

> *"I have told you these things, so that in me you may have peace. In this world you will have trouble. But take heart! I have overcome the world." (John 16:33)*

Purpose

> *He has shown you, O mortal, what is good. And what does the Lord require of you? To act justly and to love mercy and to walk humbly with your God. (Micah 6:8)*

Seeking God

> *Whoever finds their life will lose it, and whoever loses their life for my sake will find it. (Matthew 10:39)*

Stress

> *Do not be anxious about anything, but in every situation, by prayer and petition, with thanksgiving, present your requests to God. (Philippians 4:6)*

Suffering

> *Consider it pure joy, my brothers and sisters, whenever you face trials of many kinds, because you know that the testing of your faith produces perseverance. Let perseverance finish its work so that you may be mature and complete, not lacking anything. (James 1:2-4)*

Worry and Trust

The Lord is my strength and my shield; my heart trusts in him, and he helps me. My heart leaps for joy, and with my song I praise him. (Psalm 28:7)

CHAPTER 24

DISCUSSION QUESITONS

*D*iscuss the following questions with the men's ministry team to gain greater perspective together.

Section 1 Questions

– Talk about your experiences with prior men's ministries. What did you like most about them? Least? Why?

– What do you want to see happen as a result of this ministry?

– What—if any—concerns do you have as a volunteer in this ministry?

Section 2 Questions

– Of the Nine Non-Negotiables found in Chapter 3, which two or three need to be top priorities in our ministry right now? Why?

– What do you wish could be the focus for your men in the short-term? Long-term?

– Describe a small group leader you've known who was especially effective? What qualities made them stand out? What lessons can you apply to your current role in men's ministry?

Section 3 Questions

- Describe someone (no names!) who's been a challenge in a small group setting. What was the challenge and how did you deal with it? If you had it to do again, what if anything would you change about your response?

- How will you go about reinforcing the message of confidentiality in your men's ministry?

- How will your group deal with the issue of sexual purity? Who, if anyone, is the point-man to have conversations about that issue?

- What are three service projects or events you'd like your men to tackle?

- Discuss how you think you're wired for ministry. What's your love language? What spiritual gifts and skills do you bring? What do you consider your strengths and weaknesses?

- How will your group handle new visitors to your group? How will you evaluate how welcoming you are and continue to be?

CHAPTER 25

RECOMMENDED RESOURCES

Resources to address pornography:

Every Man's Battle: Winning the War on Sexual Temptation One Victory at a Time by Fred Stoekter, Mike Yorkey, Stephen Arterburn (Waterbrook, 2009)

Covenant Eyes: covenanteyes.com

Pure Desire: puredesire.org

Sexaholics Anonymous: sa.org

Video curriculums:

Epic: The Story God is Telling, Live DVD by John Eldredge

Crazy Love DVD by Francis Chan

The Way of a Worshiper DVD by Buddy Owens

Uprising DVD Kit by Erwin McManus

Romans by Tommy Nelson

Fathering Resources

Raising a Modern Day Knight: A Father's Role in Guiding His Son to Authentic Manhood by Robert Lewis (Focus on the Family, 2007)

Better Dads, Stronger Sons: How Fathers Can Guide Boys to Become Men of Character by Rick Johnson (Revell, 2006)

The Good Dad: Becoming the Father You Were Meant to Be by Jim Daly (Zondervan, 2014)

You Have What It Takes by John Eldredge by John Eldredge (Thomas Nelson, 2009)

ABOUT THE CONTRIBUTORS

Thank you to these fellow men-in-arms who generously shared their wisdom and ministry expertise:

Dr. TJ Ammons is a pastor, men's ministry leader, marriage counselor, and founder of Fight Plan (www.fightplan.org), which helps train and equip Christians in discipleship, marriage, and evangelism.

Chris Donald is passionate about sharing the love of Christ and seeing others do the same — no matter the setting. He co-founded 33rd Company (www.33rdcompany.org) to take the gospel everywhere, even dangerous places, and to equip the everyday believer to win the lost and make disciples daily. You can find some excellent training and resources on his website.

David Dusek is the founder of Rough Cut Men Ministries (www.roughcutmen.org), which is a live, interactive men's experience using a strategic combination of action movie sequences, real world current events, Biblical truth, and fireteam-sized discussion times with one objective: To get men talking about what's really going on in their lives. Check out his blog for insights into men's ministry.

And a special thanks to the men's ministry leaders who fought by my side in the 10+ years of *Wildmen*: **Jan Broucinek, Jerry Batista, Andrew Hobbs,** and **Mark Woods.** Your experience and insight helped shape this book and the lives of hundreds of men.

Author

Eric Jaqua by day is a digital marketing professional in the Information Technology and Security industry. Eric has been in youth, music or men's ministry for more than 40 years. His passion for men's ministry was ignited when God introduced him to a home group of men that grew to become a multi-campus ministry with hundreds of men in the Tampa Bay area and beyond.

Content Editor

Mikal Keefer is a Christian writer who has published more than 35 books for children, youth, and adults, as well as writing for a wide array of magazines and curricula. His input and coaching, along with his decades of experience as ministry leader, small group facilitator, were instrumental in the completion of this book.

Series Project Manager

Matt Lockhart spent more than twenty-five years serving in a variety of editorial and leadership roles in Christian publishing at Serendipity House, Group, and Standard/David C. Cook. With a penchant for book series development, he enjoys helping to create Kingdom-focused resources like the *Outreach Ministry Guides*.

Names   Phone and Email

_____   _____

_____   _____

_____   _____

_____   _____

_____   _____

_____   _____

_____   _____

_____   _____

_____   _____

Names   Phone and Email

_____   _____

_____   _____

_____   _____

_____   _____

_____   _____

_____   _____

_____   _____

_____   _____

How Can a Prayer Ministry Transform Your Church?

Whether you are part of your church's prayer ministry, or thinking about starting or joining a prayer ministry team, the *Prayer Ministry Volunteer Handbook* is for you!

We are often very quick to say we will pray for someone when we hear they are going through tough times, but do we actually follow through with our promise to pray for them? How many times do we turn to prayer only in times of crisis, as a last resort, or simply to ask things of God?

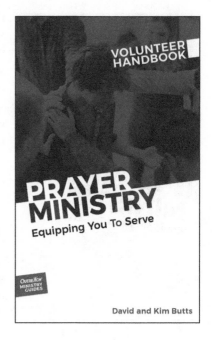

We need to make prayer the first course of action, guiding all of our life decisions. We must challenge ourselves to move beyond the dinnertime and bedtime prayers and progress to a thoughtful conversation with Christ.

Join authors David and Kim Butts as they explore how a well-equipped church prayer ministry team can serve as a model and an encouragement to support the members of the congregation, and even the pastoral staff, in their prayer journeys. Discover how you can make your church a house of prayer for all believers.

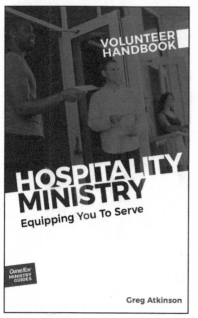

Be Our Guest

Whether you are a volunteer in your church's guest services ministry, or thinking about serving alongside ushers, greeters, welcome desk hosts, and parking lot attendants at your church, the *Hospitality Ministry Volunteer Handbook* is for you!

How does a member of community see your church? When they hear your church's name, what is their initial reaction? We want any individual who steps foot onto our church campus to immediately feel Christ's love through our actions toward them—the question is, are we doing a good job at accomplishing that mission?

We might not think of customer service and church hospitality in the same vein, but this book shows how a service mentality can make life-changing first impressions on newcomers. It's filled with specific, practical strategies and tools to help the hospitality ministry team show the love of Christ to every visitor.

Join author Greg Atkinson as he helps identify ways your church can increase its hospitality to the community around you, and, ultimately, reach those people for the Kingdom of God.

Practical Outreach Ideas and Ministry Tools

Never has there been a greater need to share the good news of God's love with those in our communities. This compact handbook shows how individual Christians and ministry teams can share the gospel by reaching out to and serving others.

Featuring 121 outreach ideas, this book helps to equip ministry teams with practical tools to serve families, children, youth, seniors, first responders, the oppressed and under resourced, millennials, single parents, local schools and businesses and more!

Designed for ministry volunteers, the book is a compact handbook of outreach ministry helps, which in addition to the dozens of outreach ideas also include outreach Scriptures and prayers, ways to share your faith, team discussion questions and recommended outreach ministries and resources.

This helpful little book is a great resource for equipping outreach ministry volunteers to serve others and to share the good news!

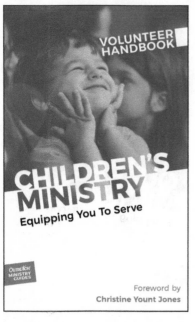

Equipping Children's Ministry Volunteers

Whether you are part of your church's children's ministry, or thinking about serving in children's ministry, the *Children's Ministry Volunteer Handbook* is for you!

Too often, people view children's ministry as a place to drop off the kids so the adults can listen to the sermon, uninterrupted. They fail to see the power and potential of children's ministry.

In Matthew 19:13-14, Jesus said, "Let the little children come to me, and do not hinder them, for the kingdom of heaven belongs to such as these." While we may see the naivete of children as a detriment, Jesus sees it as a strength—there is beauty in the simplicity of the gospel. Investing in children's ministry is a worthwhile and crucial part of the church.

This practical handbook features insights from six authors, all experts in the field of children's ministry, with over 100 years of combined experience. They will help guide you through the challenges and joys of children's ministry—and how it is vital to the Kingdom of God.

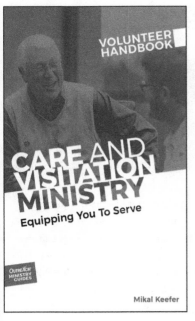

VOLUNTEER HANDBOOK

CARE AND VISITATION MINISTRY

Equipping You To Serve

OUTREACH MINISTRY GUIDES

Mikal Keefer

Talk About More Than the Weather

You've driven to the hospital and stand outside a patient's room, ready to knock and ask permission to enter. But then what? How do you make a visit that actually matters?

Here are hundreds of practical tips gleaned from the experience of veteran visitors—chaplains, pastors, and volunteers who've made thousands of visits in hospitals, nursing care facilities, rehab centers, homes, hospice centers, even prisons.

They share what to do, what not to do, and how to connect in caring, compassionate ways with people who may be experiencing the worst days of their lives.

Discover how to make visits that matter—that literally change lives—as you carry the love of Jesus to those who are sick, lonely, or simply curious about the Kingdom.

VOLUNTEER
HANDBOOK

SMALL
GROUP
MINISTRY
Equipping You To Serve

OUTREACH
MINISTRY
GUIDES

Mikal Keefer

Equip Small Group Leaders to Lead Well

Your church's small group ministry is where faith can get real. Where masks can slide off and honest struggles and doubts surface.

Maybe. It all depends on the leaders of your groups.

Give your leaders the training they need to take group members deeper. To create group cultures that encourage transparency. To cope with questions, deal with doubts, and make disciples.

This book offers your team a lifetime of easy-to-read, easy-to-remember advice from experienced small group ministry leaders. They share what they've learned, what they wish they'd known earlier, and dozens of proven practical tips that will aid in developing healthy small groups in your church.

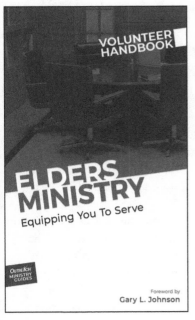

Biblical Guidance and Practical Advice for Church Elders and Prospective Elders

Equip church elders to lead well. More than better methods, the church today needs better leaders. But too often we recruit these leaders (the New Testament calls them *elders*) without equipping them for their vital task. This practical handbook presents the need, lifts up the Bible's vision for elder ministry, and provides a wealth of practical how-to training to help elders provide the spiritual leadership that can't come from anyone else. Elder teams will build unity and confidence as they discuss it together.

Written by the ministry founders and leaders of e2: effective elders, content is based on decades of local-church experience and interaction with everyday elders in hundreds of congregations.

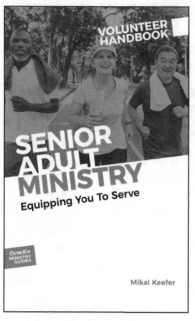

VOLUNTEER HANDBOOK

SENIOR ADULT MINISTRY
Equipping You To Serve

OUTREACH MINISTRY GUIDES

Mikal Keefer

Take your Senior Adult Ministry to the Next Level

That's what will happen when you train and equip your Senior Adult Ministry volunteers not just to minister to seniors, but also to minister *with* them. Help deepen seniors' faith and grow their friendships with one another, your team, and with God.

If your church is like most, seniors are mostly on the sidelines, but not by choice! They're hungry for purpose and fellowship. But unless you're actively creating opportunities for connection and contribution, many senior adults feel unneeded and unwelcome and simply drop out.

In this Outreach Ministry Guide you'll discover:
- Dozens of senior-friendly programming ideas
- Guidance and biblical wisdom for helping seniors cope with change, loneliness, and grief
- Ideas for energizing senior adult Sunday school classes, senior-sized service projects, and more!